GAME DAY
WISCONSIN FOOTBALL

Ron Dayne poses with his Heisman Trophy.

GAME DAY
WISCONSIN FOOTBALL

The Greatest Games, Players, Coaches and Teams
in the Glorious Tradition of Badger Football

TRIUMPH
B O O K S

Athlon® Sports™
AMERICA'S PREMIER SPORTS ANNUALS

Library of Congress Control Number: 2007901135

This book is available in quantity at special discounts for your group or organization. For further information, contact:

Triumph Books
542 South Dearborn Street
Suite 750
Chicago, Illinois 60605
(312) 939-3330
Fax (312) 663-3557

CONTRIBUTING WRITER: Tom Mulhern

EDITOR: Rob Doster

PHOTO EDITOR: Tim Clark
ASSISTANT PHOTO EDITOR: Danny Murphy

DESIGN: Eileen Wagner
PRODUCTION: Patricia Frey

PHOTO CREDITS: Athlon Sports Archive, AP/Wide World Photos, University of Wisconsin

Printed in China

ISBN: 978-1-60078-015-8

Contents

Joe Thomas

Foreword

by Pat Richter

In a hotly contested game in November 1962, the University of Wisconsin Badgers defeated the University of Minnesota Gophers at Camp Randall Stadium to earn a trip to Pasadena and the 1963 Rose Bowl.

A UW professor and former band member was asked by his children if they were going to make the trip to California and follow the Badgers. He replied that since the Badgers were in the Rose Bowl frequently (they had gone in 1953 and 1960), they wouldn't be making the trip but instead would be buying a new television set and would go the next time. Well, that gentleman and his family had to wait 31 years for the Badgers to go to another Rose Bowl!

The 1963 Rose Bowl has been considered one of the most exciting Rose Bowl games in that it matched No. 1 USC vs. No. 2 Wisconsin and went right down to the last play. For Badger fans it's been a difficult burden to carry for so many years—Wisconsin's most memorable football game had been a loss to USC, 42–37.

That all changed in the 1994 Rose Bowl when the underdog Badgers, coached by Barry Alvarez, beat UCLA 21–16. Alvarez led the Badgers to two more Rose Bowl victories in 1999 and 2000, in games that featured 1999 Heisman Trophy winner Ron Dayne.

University of Wisconsin football has a proud tradition dating back to the late 1890s and the days of the famed "Kangaroo Kicker," Pat O'Dea,

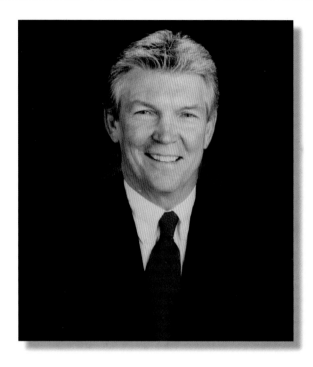

Wisconsin's first All-American in 1898. There have been other noteworthy gridiron heroes like Dave Schreiner, Elroy "Crazylegs" Hirsch, the 1951 "Hardrocks" and 1954 Heisman Trophy winner Alan "the Horse" Ameche, to name a few.

In the 30 years following the 1963 Rose Bowl game the Badgers played in only three postseason bowls and were not able to elevate their program to be consistently competitive with the upper echelon of the Big Ten, let alone the "Big Two"—Michigan and Ohio State.

The unexpected death of head coach Dave McClain in the spring of 1986 was followed by several unsuccessful replacements until Barry Alvarez was hired in 1990. Alvarez did not achieve break-even seasons in his first three years but hit the jackpot in 1993. His Badger team beat Michigan State in Tokyo, Japan, in

December 1993 to capture the Big Ten crown and the trip to Pasadena for the 1994 Rose Bowl game against UCLA.

After an absence of 31 years, Badger fans flocked to the game in droves and far outstripped the ticket allotment for the school. It was estimated that almost 70 percent of the Rose Bowl at game time was filled with Badger fans.

The Badgers won that game, and subsequently, Alvarez's teams went on to win back-to-back Rose Bowls in 1999 and 2000. In addition, throughout the 1990s and up to 2006, the Badgers were consistently competitive and were regulars on the postseason bowl scene.

Alvarez stepped down as head coach in 2006 and turned the reins over to his defensive coordinator, Bret Bielema, who at age 36 became one of the youngest head coaches in the nation. He proceeded to win 11 regular-season games with only a single loss and then took the Badgers to the Capital One Bowl in Orlando and beat Arkansas for a school-record 12-win season. He was named Big Ten Coach of the Year for his efforts.

In 2007, 44 years after the 1963 Rose Bowl, Badger fans have justifiable pride in the success and strength of Wisconsin football. The program is in good hands with a future that is brighter than ever and a mind-set that it can and will compete for the Big Ten championship and a January 1 bowl bid on a regular basis.

And Badger fans? They'd much rather follow the Badgers, tailgate and have a good time than watch it on a new television!

Introduction

The images are unforgettable and too numerous to count.

Barry Alvarez, stalking the sidelines, restoring pride to the Badger program with equal parts brashness and confidence, and delivering Rose Bowl titles to Madison. Alan "the Horse" Ameche, combining speed and power into a devastating package. Ron Dayne, barreling toward paydirt like a runaway truck. A packed Camp Randall Stadium giving full-throated support to the red and white. Championships won. Legends created.

We're distilling the pageantry and drama of Wisconsin football into the pages that follow. It's a daunting task. Few college football programs in the country inspire the loyalty and passion that the Badger football program exacts from its fans—and with good reason.

The numbers alone are impressive: two Heisman Trophy winners. Eleven championships in the toughest conference in football. Back-to-back Rose Bowl wins for the first time in Big Ten history.

But numbers alone don't do justice to the greatness of Wisconsin football. With its commitment to homegrown excellence, the Badger program has knit itself into the fabric of the entire state. Ron Smith, author of *Every Saturday in Autumn*, put it this way: "The thing that really stands out about Wisconsin is how the team is just such an integral part of the community there. In a lot of ways, Camp Randall is what college football is all about."

Through the words and images we present, we hope we have captured the true flavor of Badger football. Decades have passed since players first donned the red and white, but one thing hasn't changed: Wisconsin football is an unmatched tradition, a legacy of greatness, a way of life in the Badger State.

Lee Evans

The Greatest Players

Wisconsin's roster of greats reads like a Murderer's Row of Big Ten greats. There have been roughly 2,000 letterwinners, 185 first-team All–Big Ten Conference selections, more than 20 consensus All-Americans and more than 200 players who went on to make a roster on a professional football team, going into the 2007 season. The names are familiar to fans of college football, and for the fans of the Badgers' rivals, they still bring a shiver of dread.

Wisconsin has had so many great players that they can't all be included here, which is why the following list should be considered representative, not definitive.

They came from different eras, different cultures and different parts of the country. They also played different positions.

Yet, Alan Ameche and Ron Dayne had more in common than being the only Heisman Trophy winners in University of Wisconsin history.

Ameche, a fullback, and Dayne, a tailback, were big, strong, tough runners with deceptive speed. Both pushed the boundaries for conventional size at their positions.

As a freshman, the 6' Ameche weighed 205 pounds, and when he graduated, he was a rock-solid 212 and had to have special shoulder pads to fit his frame.

The 5'10" Dayne played much of his career around 260 pounds and was viewed by many recruiters in high school as a fullback.

Both Ameche and Dayne led their teams to Big Ten titles, had dominating performances in the Rose Bowl and became legendary figures among Badger fans.

They were also fathers, as well as student-athletes. Teammates praised their devotion to the team, despite the fact that they were the stars.

They also helped elevate Wisconsin football to a national prominence and recognition not seen before. Both also maintained their humble personalities, even though both left school as the leading rusher in Division I-A history.

Wisconsin has seen a lot of remarkable football players since the school first fielded a team in 1889. But there have been only two Heisman Trophy winners: Ameche won his in 1954, and Dayne duplicated the feat in 1999.

RON DAYNE

1996–1999, tailback
1999 Heisman Trophy
5'10", 252 pounds, Berlin, New Jersey
It began with an embrace.

The first time Wisconsin football coach Barry Alvarez met Ron Dayne during the recruiting process, the two men hugged when they finished talking. An instant bond was formed.

Alvarez, who relished the running game and the physical players it took to move the ball on the ground, had found the perfect embodiment of that philosophy in Dayne, a bruising tailback from Berlin, New Jersey, with the quick feet of a smaller back.

So, it was only fitting, on a magical evening at Camp Randall Stadium in the final regular-season game against Iowa in 1999, when Dayne became the NCAA Division I-A career rushing leader with 6,397 yards, that the two men came together on the sidelines for another hug.

Alvarez, who was unable to be on the sidelines after undergoing knee replacement surgery earlier in the season, watched from the press box as Dayne rumbled into the record books on a 31-yard run in the second quarter on a play called "23 zone," a staple of the Wisconsin running game.

It was a classic Dayne run, elegant in its simplicity, allowing him to surpass the career record of 6,279 yards set by Ricky Williams of Texas the year before. The play was designed to go to the left, although Dayne had the option of going wherever he found the hole.

Alvarez always said Dayne's best attribute was his vision. He was adept at seeing the field and finding the right holes, which was essential in the Badgers' zone-blocking scheme. In this case, the hole was over right guard.

Dayne juked the free safety, then ran over a cornerback, displaying his impressive combination of elusiveness and power, before being dragged down in front of the Wisconsin bench.

"It would not have been appropriate for (the record run) to be a two-yard gain, a little mush into the middle," Alvarez said. "One of our base plays we put in the first day (of fall camp) where he reads it, makes the cut to a seam and then comes out the back end, runs through a couple tackles.

"I thought that was very appropriate. The only thing that would have been better is if he'd have gone to the end zone with it."

Even more meaningful to Dayne than that run was the moment he shared with Alvarez, who made his way down to the sidelines in the final minutes of the game.

"The moment I most remember is probably when Coach came down on the field and I got to hug Coach and say, 'We finally got it done,'" Dayne said.

Indeed they did. Dayne was the signature player in Alvarez's 16 years as head coach, leading the Badgers to back-to-back Big Ten Conference championships and consecutive Rose Bowl wins.

"Ron really exemplified our program," Alvarez said. "I don't think there's a player that has ever meant more to a program. He's what our program is all about...blue-collar, tough, hard-nosed. He doesn't do it the easy way, but he does what you have to do for wins."

With Dayne operating behind a massive offensive line, made up mostly of homegrown players, Alvarez had a punishing, ball-control offense that wore defenses down and controlled games. It was not always pretty, and it was a style that sometimes drew derisive comments from national commentators for being boring, but it worked.

Although many colleges viewed Dayne as a fullback, Alvarez and his coaching staff always believed he was a tailback. Still, there were some reservations when Dayne showed up for his first day of summer conditioning weighing 272 pounds. Those reservations quickly vanished on one of the first days, when players were timed in 10- and 20-yard bursts.

"(Dayne) was ahead of all the running backs, just out of the blocks," running-backs coach Brian White said. "I said, 'This guy can carry the weight. He's going to be something special.'"

There was no way of knowing at the time just how special Dayne would become, although it didn't take him long to make a big impact.

The Badgers had a returning 1,000-yard rusher in 1996 in Carl McCullough, and the coaches brought Dayne along slowly at first, but after the 18-year-old freshman came off the bench to rush for his first 100-yard game against Penn State in the Big Ten Conference opener, it became clear a new chapter in the school's history was opening.

The only problem was how to tell McCullough, a player the coaches greatly admired. So, White put it as simply and as forcefully as he could.

"I have one yard to get and my life is on the line," White said he told McCullough. "There's a gun up against my head, and they say, 'Get the yard and you live. Don't get the yard and you die.' I'm putting the ball in Ron Dayne's hands."

Dayne became a national phenomenon as a freshman, despite not starting until the fifth game, rushing for 1,863 yards (not counting the bowl game), to break Herschel Walker's freshman mark of 1,616 yards.

He rushed for a school-record 339 yards at Hawaii, when defenders started diving at his feet and lost the will to tackle him in the second half. He followed that with 246 yards against Utah in the Copper Bowl, giving him 2,109 yards for the season, which at the time was eighth-best in NCAA history.

The selfless Dayne never liked the attention. He was not comfortable in the spotlight, detested talking about records and individual accomplishments and preferred the focus be on the team.

Although he was plagued by minor injuries the following two years, he still rushed for 1,457 yards as a sophomore and 1,525 as a junior. One of his best performances came in the 1999 Rose Bowl, when he rushed for 246 yards and four touchdowns as the Badgers upset UCLA 38–31.

Fans rejoiced after Dayne decided to return to UW for his senior year. The decision was vintage Dayne. It wasn't so much about the chance to set more records as it was to spend more time with his daughter, Jada. "I am having a lot of fun in college, and I wasn't ready to leave my daughter yet," Dayne said in his announcement on December 21, 1998. "Her mother is staying for her senior year (at UW), and I wanted to see my daughter and see her."

That set the stage for the dramatic senior year. Dayne needed 1,717 yards to pass Williams, and billboards with that number went up around Madison before the season. "It looked insurmountable to me," said Alia Lester, who was Dayne's girlfriend at the time and the mother of his child. "It looked very intimidating. I just thought, 'I'm not going to think

"Because we get a ring for that. I just get my name on the books for breaking the record."
—TAILBACK RON DAYNE, SAYING A SECOND STRAIGHT TRIP TO THE ROSE BOWL
ECLIPSED THE ACCOMPLISHMENT OF BREAKING THE NCAA DIVISION I-A
RUSHING RECORD AGAINST IOWA ON NOVEMBER 13, 1999.

about it because look how many yards (he needs).' You really had to have an exceptional season to get all that."

Dayne made it look easy. Despite getting pulled early by Alvarez in a number of blowouts, which caused a minor controversy in the local media, Dayne came into the Iowa game needing only 99 yards to break the record.

He surpassed that in the first half on his way to 216 yards in the game. More importantly, the Badgers won 41–3 for the outright Big Ten title and a second straight berth in the Rose Bowl.

Dayne closed his career with another sterling performance in the Rose Bowl, rushing for 200 yards in a 17–9 win over Stanford.

He became the school's second Heisman Trophy winner in dominating fashion, with a better than 2-to-1 margin in the voting. Georgia Tech senior quarterback Joe Hamilton was a distant second and Virginia Tech redshirt freshman quarterback Michael Vick finished third. That gave Dayne a sweep of all the major awards for his position that season, having earlier won the Walter Camp, Maxwell and Doak Walker.

"I'm just happy and honored and blessed," said Dayne, a man of many yards and few words.

Dayne was a first-round draft pick of the New York Giants, but like many other Heisman winners, he wasn't able to duplicate his college success in the NFL. He rushed for 770 yards as a rookie and 690 his second year, but things declined rapidly after that, and he bounced to the Denver Broncos and then the Houston Texans in 2006.

The most memorable moment from Dayne's career had to be the scene after the Iowa game—which was also one of the most spine-tingling moments in Camp Randall Stadium history.

Dayne stood on a podium in the middle of the field after the game, as the fans who adored him for four years held aloft white

RON DAYNE'S 1999 SEASON

OPP.	ATT.	YARDS	AVG.	TD	LONG
Murray State	20	135	6.8	3	26
Ball State	31	158	5.1	1	19
at Cincinnati	28	231	8.3	1	29
Michigan (#4)	22	88	4.0	1	34
at Ohio State (#12)	32	161	5.0	4	46
at Minnesota (#25)	25	80	3.2	1	16
Indiana	17	167	9.8	2	69
Michigan State (#11)	34	214	6.3	2	51
at Northwestern	35	162	4.6	2	24
at Purdue (#17)	32	222	6.9	1	41
Iowa	27	216	8.0	1	38
Stanford (#22)	34	200	5.9	1	64
Totals	337	2,034	6.0	20	69

CAREER RUSHING TOTALS

1996	325	2,109	6.5	21	71
1997	263	1,457	5.5	15	80
1998	295	1,525	5.2	15	54
1999	337	2,034	6.0	20	69
Totals	1,220	7,125	5.8	71	80

towels with No. 33 printed on
them. Athletic Director Pat Richter
was moved to tears, and Dayne
smiled broadly during a surprise
ceremony in which "Dayne 33"
was revealed on the facade of the
stadium's upper deck.

"I didn't know what to say,"
Dayne said. "I was just so happy
and grateful. I'm still kind of
amazed and dazed."

The same could be said of his
coach, who, after making his way
to the sidelines near the end of the
game, finally reached Dayne for an
emotional embrace. They were two
men, near the end of an incredible
journey, who believed in each other
and what they were doing and let
nothing stand in their way.

"Ron's been a special player to
me," Alvarez said. "I think we've
had a very good bond. First time I
met him, I hugged him. So, I think
it was only appropriate I hug him
when he broke the record and we
accomplished what we did.

"How can you forget that big
smile? He just lit it up. I went
down on the sidelines and you see
him smiling and trying to work
his way over to me, it was very
meaningful and something you
always have—that picture in your
mind."

ALAN AMECHE
1951–1954, fullback
1954 Heisman Trophy
6'0", 220 pounds, Kenosha, Wisconsin

Debate swirled regarding the origin of Alan "the Horse" Ameche's famous nickname, with conflicting reports and various people, including two Badger assistant coaches, taking credit for it.

Tom Braatz, a former NFL personnel director with the Green Bay Packers and Miami Dolphins, grew up in Kenosha, Wisconsin, with Ameche and played against his close friend in college and the NFL.

"He got the nickname 'Horse' from the players because he was kind of built like a racehorse, very strong physically but with very skinny, long legs," Braatz said.

A Kenosha news sportswriter once compared Ameche during his high school days to Citation, the great racehorse, although, truth be told, Ameche was more like a plow horse.

The most popular story traces the nickname to the first time in 1951 when the Wisconsin freshmen, including Ameche, scrimmaged against the varsity and "sideliners watched him bolt through the tough varsity line," according to a Wisconsin press release.

Some reports credited Bob Odell, a Badgers assistant, with coming up with the nickname after watching Ameche's high step. "That boy is a horse, a human horse who runs," Odell was quoted as saying.

Several reports mentioned Ameche's running style—his knees coming up high and his arms flailing as he roared into the line—with the exact same words, "high-stepping and sunfishing like a mean rodeo bronco," although no source for that phrase was mentioned.

Finally, George Lanphear, the Badgers freshman coach, also liked to take credit for coming up with the nickname and supposedly had this exchange on the sidelines with *Wisconsin State Journal* sportswriter Hank McCormick:

Lanphear: "There goes that Ameche again, working like a horse."

McCormick: "You mean, he runs like a horse."

Whatever the case, the nickname fit. Unlike other fullbacks at the time, who usually lowered their heads, Ameche almost always went into the line with his head straight up. With those high-churning knees and impressive strength and power, he was extremely difficult to tackle.

While his running style might have been unique, it was effective. As one sportswriter at the time put it, "Everything he hits falls down. Nothing fancy about his style. He gets the ball and bang!—he plows right over you."

He was born Lino Dante Amici in Italy in 1933. The family changed the spelling of the last name after moving to this country. Lino didn't think his first name was rugged enough, so at age 16 he changed it to Alan.

Nobody questioned his toughness after that, although it had nothing to do with his name. There was an often-repeated story that in 1949, Ameche entered a Golden Gloves novice championship as a light heavyweight and ended up winning the title. By default. His opponents heard he had entered, and every one of them dropped out. Such was Ameche's reputation in that part of the state.

But a report in Ameche's hometown newspaper sounded more truthful. It said Ameche knocked out his first opponent, and the next scheduled rival didn't show up.

His parents, August and Elizabeth Ameche, immigrated to the United States not once, but twice. They returned to Italy for one year in between, with young Lino, at age four, wearing the youth fascist uniform prescribed at the time by Mussolini, something Ameche neither remembered nor wished to discuss in later years. The family settled in Kenosha, where August got work in a factory.

The football teams at Mary Bradford High School, referred to as Kenosha High School at the time in newspaper accounts, were lousy until Chuck Jaskwich, a former quarterback at Notre Dame, showed up before Ameche's junior year and whipped everybody into shape.

As a senior, Bradford had one of the best prep football teams in Wisconsin history, and Ameche was an all-state fullback. Nine of 11 starters on that team went on to play college football. The only opponent to put up a fight was Madison East, which led 13–0 at halftime. Ameche scored three touchdowns in the second half on runs of 15, 39 and 41 yards to carry his team to an 18–13 victory.

Ameche earned six letters in football and track and field and was a Class A state champion in the shot put as a junior and finalist in the state meet in the 100-yard dash.

He was the subject of an intense recruiting battle that lent itself to almost as many stories as the nickname. Most people in Wisconsin assumed he would go to Notre Dame, since that is where his prep coach played. Just to be safe, Fred Miller, a Notre Dame captain in 1928 and the owner of Milwaukee's Miller

Brewing Company, pressured Ameche to sign with the Fighting Irish.

One story Ameche apparently later told his friends is Miller waved a $1,500 check in front of his mother and hinted that the family, which did not have much money, would receive that sum if her son signed with Notre Dame. The ploy apparently backfired because Alan became enraged that such pressure was being exerted on his family.

There was reportedly even a phone call from Don Ameche, the Hollywood actor and radio star, urging Alan to go to Notre Dame. Don Ameche was frequently referred to as a "distant cousin" or "second cousin," but Alan told the *Kenosha News* they were not related.

Wisconsin fans reportedly formed a committee to keep Ameche home and threatened a boycott of Miller beer. In the end, Ameche simply decided he wanted to stay close to home. It also helped that Badger coach Ivy Williamson recruited four or five of his prep teammates to also play at Wisconsin.

"I respected Notre Dame, but I figured it would be better if I stayed home and went to my state university with a lot of the boys I played with at Kenosha High," Ameche was quoted as saying in a 1988 story in *The* [Baltimore] *Sun.*

Despite the fanfare surrounding Ameche and the expectations raised by his first scrimmage against the varsity, he didn't start his first junior varsity game against Iowa on September 28, 1951. But he dominated after getting in the game and scored two touchdowns.

That was the year the rule was relaxed, allowing freshmen to play on the varsity, and Ameche dressed for the varsity game the following day but carried the ball only once. The Badgers had an outstanding fullback in Jim Hammond, who was not only a captain but was also expected to be a first-team All–Big Ten selection.

Ameche played against Illinois the following week and replaced Hammond as the starter a week later against Ohio State. By his fourth game, he proved himself by rushing for 148 yards against Purdue and started nearly every game after that in his college career.

"You could tell how good he was by the fact that he played as a freshman and beat out Jim Hammond, a good fullback," Clarence Stensby, an offensive guard and another member of the 1951 freshman class, told the *Wisconsin State Journal* in 1994. "We took him for granted. We didn't know how good he really was. He wasn't a guy who blew his own horn. He went both ways the last two years, yet he never complained.

"When you laid a good block for him, he was always complimentary. He never complained (if you missed a block). The success of our halfbacks was due to Al. We had a counter play, a buck lateral. The quarterback stuck the ball in Al's stomach and then flipped it out to the halfback. He always ran that hard."

Ameche was the first freshman to lead the Big Ten in rushing, gaining 774 yards in 147 attempts, both conference records. Including non-conference games, he set a school record with 824 rushing yards.

He may have been at his best during the last four regular-season games in 1952, with 99 carries for 551 yards and five touchdowns, helping UW clinch its first Rose Bowl berth. He lived up to enormous expectations in the Rose Bowl against USC, rushing for 133 yards on 28 carries. However, he was caught from behind on a 54-yard run early in the third quarter, and the Trojans won 7–0. Ameche became the first Wisconsin back to top 1,000 rushing yards, finishing the season with 1,079.

That was also a big year for Ameche's personal life. He married his high school sweetheart, Yvonne Molinaro, on Thanksgiving. They had their first two of six children while Ameche was playing for Wisconsin.

The free substitution rule was changed the following year, and players were forced to go both ways. Ameche also played linebacker for the first time, and his rushing numbers fell off the last two years. But he also drew praise for his play on defense, and, after playing as many as 55 minutes in a game, his nickname briefly expanded to "the Iron Horse."

With every defense the Badgers faced geared to stop Ameche, Williamson devised an offense with quarterback Jim Miller operating like a single wing tailback to reduce the pressure on Ameche. Miller ran for six touchdowns and threw for six more that season and was the Big Ten's passing leader.

Ameche was one of college football's most decorated players his final two years. He was named to 10 All-America rosters his junior year and was on the first team of six of them. After struggling with his grades when he first arrived at the university, Ameche earned Academic All-America honors his final two years.

His senior year was his worst statistical year; he finished with 641 yards on 146 carries. He rushed for 117 yards in a 13–7 loss to Iowa in the sixth game, then picked up 65 yards early in the following game against Northwestern, before suffering a sprained ankle that bothered him the rest of the season. He didn't have a single carry against Illinois and finished with 26 yards on 13 carries in his final game, although the Badgers trounced rival Minnesota 27–0. Still, he was named an All-American, as well as the most valuable player in the Big Ten.

Ameche played in 37 games for Wisconsin and rushed 701 times for 3,345 yards, an average of 4.8 yards per carry, and 25 touchdowns. The previous record for career rushing yards was 1,748, set by fullback Ben Bendrick from 1945 to 1948. At the time, Ameche held every UW rushing record for season and single-game performances.

Since NCAA statistics did not count bowl games at the time, his NCAA career record was 3,212 yards on 673 carries.

Wisconsin guard Gary Messner, a captain in 1954, said, "He was the greatest football player I have ever seen. Nobody had to do a great deal of blocking for him. There aren't a lot of guys who could do it all, but he could."

UCLA coach Red Sanders said, "Ameche is the strongest runner in football history, not excepting Bronko Nagurski."

A crowd of more than 1,000—tickets sold out in 48 hours—turned out at the Eagles Club in Kenosha for a celebration after Ameche's senior year. Among the gifts lavished on Ameche were 3,212 $1 bills—"a buck a yard" for each of the yards he gained at Wisconsin, a new car, which had just rolled off the American Motors Corporation assembly line in town and a palomino horse.

The Heisman Trophy wasn't nearly as well-publicized back then. Ameche didn't even know he had finished in the top five the previous year. He didn't think he had much of a chance after a senior year he regarded as his worst in college. The voters thought otherwise. In an obvious nod to his four years of accomplishments, Ameche beat out such stars as center Kurt Burris of

Oklahoma and Ohio State halfback Howard "Hopalong" Cassady.

The most thrilling thing for Ameche at the time was the chance to meet his boyhood idol, Doc Blanchard of Army, the 1945 winner.

Perhaps the biggest factor in Ameche's victory was his performance in the 1953 Rose Bowl, which won over the West Coast sportswriters. After the game, a story in the *Los Angeles Times* said of Ameche, "The great Alan Ameche was just that—great."

Ameche described himself as "proud and humble" when he received the Heisman. "I know many other deserving players could have received this honor," he said.

Even with all his NFL success to follow, Ameche later regarded the Heisman as his proudest achievement. "The Heisman Trophy was the single most important award for Alan," Yvonne said in a story published in the Heisman Journal on the 50-year anniversary of her husband's award. "He treasured being part of that group of athletes, perhaps more from a camaraderie standpoint than the award itself. It meant more to him as time passed by."

After leaving school, Ameche was courted by the Canadian Professional League and offered a reported $50,000 to wrestle professionally. Instead, he entered the 1955 NFL draft and was taken, fittingly, by the Baltimore Colts—"the Horse" became a Colt—and signed for $15,000, the most the team had ever paid to a rookie.

The first time Ameche touched the ball, 25 seconds into his first NFL game, he ran 79 yards off left tackle for a touchdown against the Chicago Bears.

"The pros thought they could judge his speed, but they couldn't judge his heart," John Walsh, a Madison attorney and fomrer

Wisconsin boxing coach who helped Ameche sign his first professional contract, told the *Wisconsin State Journal*.

He led the league in rushing his first season, while being named Rookie of the Year. But his biggest run was yet to come.

In the NFL's first sudden-death overtime, in the 1958 championship game played at frozen Yankee Stadium, Ameche ran one yard over right tackle through a gaping hole for the winning touchdown, the clock reading 8:15 of the first overtime. "It's probably the shortest run I ever made, and the most remembered," Ameche said.

Ameche's NFL career ended after six seasons and 4,045 yards when he suffered a torn Achilles tendon. He played on two championship teams.

As successful as Ameche was at football, he might have been a better businessman. At a time when McDonald's was just starting to take off, Ameche and Colts teammate Gino Marchetti borrowed money and founded the Gino's Hamburgers chain. Ameche was heavily involved, down to picking out the meat, and served as corporate secretary and as a member of its board of directors. The chain had 300 locations at its peak and was eventually sold, earning Ameche an estimated $19 million.

But Ameche was not done yet. He donated time and money to a variety of worthwhile causes. One of them, while living in the Philadelphia suburb of Devon, Pennsylvania, was in arranging educational grants for inner-city children in Philadelphia and Baltimore.

Art Donovan, his former Colts teammate, told *The* [Baltimore] *Sun*, "No one ever had a bad word to say about 'the Horse.' The things he would do for people, out of the goodness of his heart, were amazing."

In 1980 Ameche was one of five men to receive the National Collegiate Athletic Association Silver Anniversary Award, given to those who led distinguished professional lives after outstanding athletic careers.

Ameche stayed loyal to Wisconsin and was generous to the athletic department. Coaches would call on him to help with recruiting. He would never tell a recruit to go to Wisconsin, only how great the school had been for him. During halftime of a game against Northwestern in 1984, he presented his Heisman Trophy to Athletic Director Elroy Hirsch as a gift to the university.

Ameche died on August 8, 1988, in Houston, Texas, of complications following heart bypass surgery. He underwent triple bypass surgery nine years earlier, and his heart had deteriorated and was unable to take the strain of a second operation. In 1996 Yvonne married Glenn Davis, "Mr. Outside," who won the Heisman Trophy in 1946 while playing for Army.

The No. 35 worn by Ameche was retired at halftime of the Michigan-Wisconsin game in 1988. He was voted to Wisconsin's All-Time team by fans in 1969 and named the school's "all-time greatest player." His name and number were added to the upper-deck facade at Camp Randall Stadium in 2000, a tradition started the year before with Ron Dayne.

"Everything was good for him," Braatz said of his old buddy, following Ameche's death. "He has been blessed, he really was, with great friends, a great wife, great business relationship and a great background in football—the whole works."

ALAN AMECHE'S 1954 SEASON

OPP.	ATT.	YARDS	AVG.	TD	LONG
Marquette	18	107	5.9	1	47
at Michigan State	17	127	7.5	1	29
Rice (#11)	21	90	4.3	2	19
Purdue (#5)	18	73	4.1	1	26
at Ohio State (#4)	16	42	2.6	0	9
at Iowa	26	117	4.5	1	22
Northwestern	17	59	3.5	1	20
at Illinois	0	0	0.0	0	0
Minnesota (#10)	13	26	2.0	2	4
Totals	146	641	4.4	9	47
CAREER TOTALS					
1951	157	824	5.2	4	64
1952	233	1,079	4.6	7	43
1953	165	801	4.8	5	41
1954	146	641	4.4	9	47
Totals	701	3,345	4.8	25	64

It's no coincidence the only Heisman Trophy winners in Wisconsin history carried the football. Of all the positions, the Badgers have the most tradition at running back.

Not only did they have two players, in Ameche and Dayne, who left school as the Division I-A career rushing leaders, but they also had a streak of 10 straight years, from 1993 to 2002, with a 1,000-yard rusher, the longest in Big Ten history and tied for second-longest in NCAA history with Southern California, trailing only the 12 straight by North Carolina from 1973 to 1984.

Ameche wasn't the school's first great fullback, either. **Marlin "Pat" Harder** was a legendary tough guy—also known as "the Mule"—from a strict Mormon family in Milwaukee, who was the Big Ten's scoring and rushing champion in 1941. He was named first-team All–Big Ten in 1941 and 1942 and was the MVP of the 1943 College All-Star Game, scoring two touchdowns.

Never a serious student, Harder had a reputation for being a "roustabout" and a "character" and liked to frequent the bars on State Street. He was also a handful for coach Harry Stuhldreher. But Harder's teammates universally respected him.

In the book *Third Down and a War to Go*, which chronicled the 1942 team that went 8–1–1 before several players left for World War II, author Terry Frei said it was the consensus on the team that Harder—not halfback Elroy Hirsch or end Dave Schreiner—was the best player on the team.

"On the field, Harder was a terror," Frei wrote. "He didn't much care if he was carrying the ball, blocking or tackling, because all he wanted to do was run over or hit somebody."

The second pick in the 1943 NFL draft, Harder led that league in scoring three times. He was elected to the College Football Hall of Fame in 1993.

Here is a look at some of the other top running backs in Wisconsin history:

Rufus Ferguson (1970–1972): The Badgers needed more than a running back in 1970. Coming off a three-year stretch in which they had a 3–26–1 record and fan interest plummeted, they also needed a headliner. They found both in the charismatic 5'6" Ferguson, who was dubbed "the Roadrunner" and celebrated touchdowns with his famous shuffle in the end zone. During his three seasons, average attendance jumped from 48,898 to 70,454. Ferguson led the Badgers in rushing all three years, and his 2,814 career yards ranked second only to Alan Ameche at the time.

Billy Marek (1972–1975): He developed his running style at Chicago's St. Rita High School, where he was told always to keep his feet moving and always fall forward. So, that is what Marek did for three prolific seasons. As a freshman, he backed up Rufus Ferguson and carried once for six yards. The next three years, he was one of the best running backs in college football, rushing for at least 1,200 yards each season. He was only 5'8", and he weighed 185 pounds. He didn't have blazing speed, but he had good quickness and could make tacklers miss. And, man, did he know how to keep those legs churning. His blockers knew if they gave him a slight crack, it was all he needed. He won the Big Ten rushing title in 1974, averaging 161

Billy Marek

yards per game, and led the nation in scoring, averaging 12.7 points per game. He rushed for 304 yards on 43 carries in the final game that year against Minnesota. "I'm always tired," Marek said afterward. "But I like to carry the ball. I knew I was going to have it a lot, but that's my job."

He was the school's all-time leading rusher with 3,709 yards and 44 touchdowns until Ron Dayne shattered both marks.

Brent Moss (1991–1994): Few players have fallen as fast or as far as Moss, the first outstanding tailback of the Barry Alvarez era. Moss was the Most Valuable Player in the first Rose Bowl victory in Wisconsin history, rushing for 158 yards on 36 carries in the 21–16 win over UCLA in 1994. He was named the Big Ten's Most Valuable Player as well that season as a junior when he rushed for 1,637

yards, which at the time was the school's single-season record. He was a punishing runner who ran "downhill," as the coaches liked to say, always finishing runs. But 11 months after his Rose Bowl performance, when he was about to become Wisconsin's all-time leading rusher, he was busted with two rocks of crack cocaine in one of his socks. He pled guilty to possession of crack cocaine, received two years probation and was kicked off the team, missing the final two regular-season games and the 1995 Hall of Fame Bowl. He finished with 3,428 career yards and was the school's No. 2 rusher at the time, but the damage was done. He went from a likely second-round draft pick to an undrafted free agent who played in four games that year with the St. Louis Rams, rushing 22 times for 90 yards.

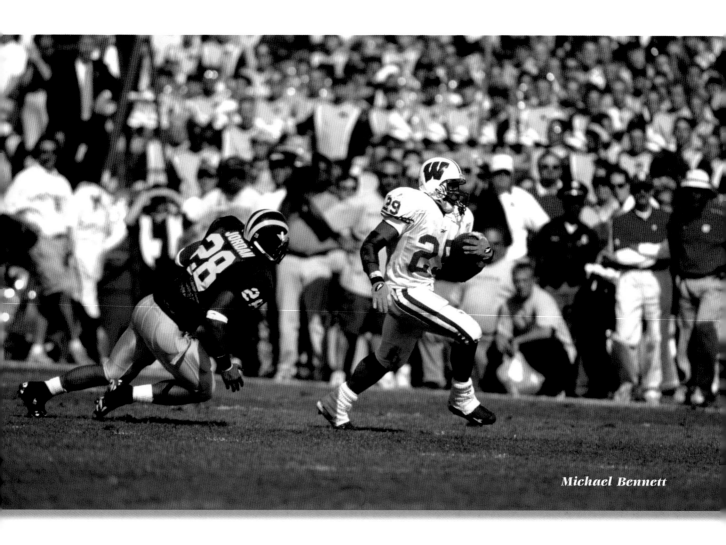

Michael Bennett

Michael Bennett (2000) and Brian Calhoun (2005): Michael Bennett and Brian Calhoun both had sensational single seasons for the Badgers. Bennett had the task of following Ron Dayne in 2000, after getting only 57 carries as Dayne's backup in 1999, his only previous season of college football.

But Bennett, an academic non-qualifier as a freshman, burst onto the national scene in his second start by rushing for 290 yards against Oregon, the fourth-highest total in UW history at the time. The speedy Bennett went on to rush for 1,681 yards in his only season as a starter, ranking third in the country with an average of 159.8 yards per game. He then declared early for the NFL draft after his junior year and was a first-round draft pick of the Minnesota Vikings. He was selected to the Pro Bowl in 2003.

Calhoun, from Oak Creek, Wisconsin, initially left the state to go to Colorado. But after two productive seasons, there was talk of moving him to wide receiver, so he transferred to Wisconsin. In 2005, he put together one of the best seasons ever by a Badger running back, finishing with 2,207 all-purpose yards, second only to Dayne's record of 2,242 yards set in 1996.

Anthony Davis (2001–2004): The Badgers went into the 2001 season scrambling to find a tailback, after Michael Bennett left for the NFL after his junior season. Davis was undersized at 5'8", 194 pounds, but he had breakaway speed and surprising power between the tackles. He quickly emerged from the pack as a redshirt freshman and held the job for most of the next four seasons. He had a remarkably productive first year, rushing for 1,466 yards, despite missing a game with a turf-toe injury. His sophomore year was even better—he rushed for 1,555 yards, and suddenly he looked to be a threat to challenge Dayne's school record of 7,125 yards (counting bowls). But ankle injuries curtailed his productivity his last two seasons. Still, he finished with 4,476 yards, good for second on the school's all-time list behind Dayne, and 42 rushing touchdowns.

Anthony Davis

When asked to describe the typical Wisconsin offensive linemen, former Badger left tackle Chris McIntosh said, "You think of a tough guy, blue-collar. There's nothing fancy about it, that's for sure. It's not the most glamorous position. I think you need somebody in there who's not afraid to stick his face in on something."

Former Notre Dame coach Lou Holtz used to say a football team's leaders should come from the offensive line, because they are some of the most selfless players on the team. Barry Alvarez coached under Holtz at Notre Dame for three years and took those words to heart as head coach of the Badgers.

The tradition of Wisconsin linemen goes back a long way before Alvarez, to players like Ken Bowman in the 1960s, Dennis Lick and Mike Webster in the 1970s and Paul Gruber in the 1980s.

But under Alvarez, the offensive linemen never went unappreciated. In fact, few places in college football celebrate offensive linemen as much as Wisconsin does. While they may not be treated like rock stars—that would have made them uncomfortable anyway—their value to the team is always praised.

McIntosh became the first UW player to start 50 games in his career and helped tailback Ron Dayne become the leading rusher in Division I-A history. So, when Dayne was asked about McIntosh before his final game, he said, "He's meant a lot to the team, probably more than me."

Alvarez knew the one thing he could find in abundance in Wisconsin—in addition to cheese and brats—was enormous offensive linemen. So, that's what he decided to build his program around. From 1993 to 2006, the Badgers had 13 offensive linemen selected in the NFL draft, and 11 came from within the state.

Not only did the offensive line produce some of the best players under Alvarez—including All-Americans like Cory Raymer, Aaron Gibson, McIntosh and Joe Thomas—but also some of the best leaders.

Alvarez frequently called tackle Joe Panos, a captain on the first Rose Bowl team in 1994, the best leader he ever had. McIntosh, who served as a captain on the next two Rose Bowl teams in 1999 and 2000, might have been a close second. Thomas also served as a two-time captain, including the 2006 season, after Alvarez retired from coaching.

"I think for many years, the offensive line (was) pretty much the leaders of the team," McIntosh said. "There's always an offensive lineman that's a captain. I don't think that's a coincidence."

It was McIntosh, more than anybody else, who set the tone for the back-to-back Rose Bowl victories. It happened shortly after the humbling 33–6 loss to Georgia in the 1998 Outback Bowl. The returning members of the team got together for their first offseason meeting, and McIntosh got up in front of the entire room.

"Here's Chris McIntosh standing up and saying, 'I didn't come here to play in the Outback Bowl or the Copper Bowl. I came here to play in the Rose Bowl. To win the Rose Bowl,'" running backs coach Brian White said.

"I'm sitting back there thinking, 'It would be one thing if we beat Georgia in the Outback Bowl. We just got beat, 33–6, and got embarrassed. But that was the expectation (McIntosh) had, that that group set for that team (in 1998).

That was the single-mindedness we had as a team...it has carried over into (1999)."

Said McIntosh: "I wanted to go to the Rose Bowl. I was recruited right after the 1994 Rose Bowl team. That's the reason I came here. It was the reason a lot of guys came here. That was one of my dreams and goals. I didn't want to be consistently playing in those (other bowls). I came here to play in big ones."

Within UW's overall tradition of linemen came another tradition of outstanding centers, which started with Bowman (1961–1963), who played for the Green Bay Packers for 10 years, starting on three NFL championship teams and becoming the first Badger to play in a Super Bowl in 1967.

But nobody compared to Webster (1971–1973), from Tomahawk, Wisconsin, one of the toughest guys to ever play the game and one of the top centers in NFL history with the Pittsburgh Steelers (1974–1988) and Kansas City Chiefs (1989–1990). Webster won four Super Bowls with the Steelers, was a nine-time Pro Bowl selection, started 150 straight games during one stretch and was voted in 2000 as a member of the All-Time NFL team. Webster is one of only two former Badgers in the Pro Football Hall of Fame, along with Elroy Hirsch.

Nobody expected that level of greatness when he arrived at UW, although Neil Graff, a senior quarterback in 1971, remembers Webster working out nonstop to squeeze everything he could from his body.

"I remember him running and working out just endlessly, lifting weights, being at the stadium virtually every day, all the time," Graff said. "He was a constant fixture over there. I don't think anybody had a clue he would rise to

Mike Webster

the levels that he did, but when you talk about a self-made player, a self-made man, he certainly was. He deserved all of the accolades and all of the honors he received because he worked so hard during his early years to achieve that high level of play."

Webster died tragically of a heart attack at age 50, and his post-football life was not easy. His family said he suffered from brain injuries as a result of his playing career, and when he was inducted into the Pro Football Hall of Fame in 1997, there were reports he was heavily in debt, living in his car and suffering from depression and memory loss.

Cory Raymer

It was almost as if Webster made the ultimate sacrifice, giving his life to play the game he loved. "He gave so much to the game that it did have an effect on his physical life after football," Graff said. "There's no doubt about that."

The center tradition was re-established under Alvarez with Cory Raymer, a two-time first-team All–Big Ten selection in 1993 and 1994 and consensus All-American in 1994, who went on to a successful NFL career with the Washington Redskins and San Diego Chargers.

He was one of four-straight Wisconsin centers to be drafted and go on to play in the NFL, followed by Derek Engler, Casey Rabach and Al Johnson.

As good as the centers have been, the list of offensive tackles is every bit as impressive. Dennis Lick was a consensus All-American in 1975 and a first-team All–Big Ten tackle in 1974 and 1975 who opened holes for Billy Marek and was a first-round pick of the Chicago Bears, going on to play six seasons in the NFL.

Paul Gruber helped usher in the age where NFL left tackles were paid almost as highly as quarterbacks. After being named an All-American in 1987, Gruber was the fourth pick overall in the 1988 draft by the Tampa Bay Buccaneers. He held out in training camp, which wasn't as common back then, before receiving a $1.25 million signing bonus and a five-year contract worth $3.8 million that made him the richest offensive lineman in the NFL. He played for 12 seasons and started all 16 games in 10 of those years, including a club-record 183 straight starts at one point. He played in three Pro Bowls.

Aaron Gibson got a lot of attention during his All-America season in 1998 because of his mammoth size. He weighed more than 400 pounds when he arrived at Wisconsin and was listed at 6'7" and 370 pounds as a senior, when he was a finalist for the Lombardi and Outland awards. But the right tackle was incredibly athletic for his size. In addition to setting most of the school weightlifting records, he had a vertical leap of 31 inches, could do the splits and could dunk a basketball.

The right tackle was also one of the most dominating run blockers the Badgers ever had. Following a 37–3 win over Illinois in which Ron Dayne rushed for 190 yards, Illini coach Ron Turner said of Gibson, "He just mauled our guys."

McIntosh set standards for durability and reliability in his career, never missing a start in four years at left tackle. He was a consensus All-American and an Outland Trophy finalist in 1999 and a first-round pick of the Seattle Seahawks, although his career was cut short after two seasons by a neck injury.

But if you are looking for the best offensive lineman in school history, at least in regards to his college career, McIntosh believes the choice is Joe Thomas, a two-time All-American and three-year starter at left tackle from 2004–2006.

The thing that separated Thomas, 6'8", 313 pounds, from many of the other top linemen who came before him was the combination of incredible athleticism and nearly flawless technique. Thomas posted a 37-inch vertical jump and ran the 40-yard dash in 4.8 seconds during his college career and was also one of the top competitors in the shot put in the Big Ten.

"The athleticism is one thing," McIntosh said. "I had the pleasure of playing with a lot of guys that were very gifted athletes. But his technique is as strong as his athleticism.

"What makes him a good player is he relies on his technique and then uses his God-given tools and what he's worked so hard for. I've seen a lot of guys play that were great athletes, that get the job done, relying on their athleticism. He can do it relying on his technique, which also makes him special."

Of course, no discussion of the Badgers' top offensive linemen would be complete without recognition of the early trailblazers. Robert "Butts" Butler was the school's first consensus All-American as a tackle in 1912, also making the second team the following year. He was a three-year letterman and a member of the school's last undefeated team, which went 7–0 in 1912. In a 14–0 victory over Minnesota in the next-to-last game, Butler and 10 teammates

Paul Gruber

Aaron Gibson

Joe Thomas

played the entire game. Butler played pro ball for the Canton Bulldogs, where he was a teammate of the legendary Jim Thorpe, and went into the College Football Hall of Fame in 1972.

Another former Badger who played with Thorpe in Canton was Howard Buck, a consensus All-America tackle in 1915 and considered by many as the best lineman of his era. He played "roving center" on defense and was credited with making half of his team's tackles. Thorpe said Buck was the finest lineman he ever played with, and after playing with the Green Bay Packers from 1921 to 1925, Buck was elected into the Packers Hall of Fame. After his playing career, he also became the first head football coach at Miami (Florida) in 1926.

Marty Below was a transfer from UW-Oshkosh, where he was a four-sport athlete after serving in World War I. He was a first-team All-American in 1923 who was described as a "rugged right tackle," who was inducted into the College Football Hall of Fame in 1988. Former Illinois standout Red Grange, one of the greatest college football players ever, once said, "Marty was the greatest lineman I ever played against."

HIRSCH AND RICHTER: TWO OF A KIND

Elroy Hirsch and Pat Richter lived almost parallel lives. They were a pair of state-born sports legends who attended the University of Wisconsin and would have long been remembered for their exploits on various playing fields.

But they were also called upon at two critical junctures, because of their charisma and know-how, to rescue UW's debt-ridden Athletic Department, serving tenures of similar length.

As a result, they are not only two of the most iconic athletes in Wisconsin history, but also two of the most important figures as well.

ELROY HIRSCH

1942, halfback
UW athletic director, 1969–1987

Elroy Hirsch used to sign autographs with the phrase, "Always a Badger," and it was clear his heart always belonged in Wisconsin.

After the popular Hirsch died of natural causes at age 80 in Madison on January 28, 2004, Wayne Esser, the executive director of a UW football booster club, was fielding telephone calls about Hirsch from newspapers from Los Angeles to small Wisconsin towns. "You could not believe how the people loved him," Esser said.

Such was the far-flung appeal of Hirsch, who appeared in three movies following his legendary football career and could fit in anywhere from Hollywood to rural Wisconsin. But Hirsch, who was born in Wausau, never lost his small-town roots that appealed so much to Wisconsin residents.

"He had that great personality, and his fame that went with it," Esser said. "People recognized him. But he was a small-town boy."

Hirsch is one of only two Badgers in the Pro Football Hall of Fame, along with Mike Webster, and was named to the NFL's all-time team as a wide receiver.

Handsome, athletic and charismatic, Hirsch was larger than life. He played only one year at UW, on the storied 1942 team, as a triple-threat halfback. But what a lasting impact he had on Wisconsin fans. The Badgers finished 8–1–1 that season and were ranked No. 3 in the final Associated Press poll.

Hirsch was given the nickname "Crazylegs" by *Chicago Daily News* sportswriter Francis Powers, who covered the Badgers' 13–7 victory over Great Lakes Naval Station in the sixth game that season. Powers wrote, "Hirsch ran like a demented duck. His crazy legs were gyrating in six different directions all at the same time during a 61-yard touchdown run that cemented the win." From that day forward, Hirsch was "Crazylegs."

His finest moment that season came in a 17–7 win over top-ranked Ohio State. He threw one touchdown pass and accounted for more than 200 yards of total offense.

That season he rushed for 786 yards, passed for 226 yards and had 390 yards receiving on the way to third-team All-America honors from *Look* magazine.

With World War II raging, Hirsch and many of his teammates entered the Marine Corps. Many of the seniors began duty right away. Dave Schreiner, an All-America end, was at Marines boot camp at Parris Island, South Carolina, by May of that year.

The undergraduate players were referred to as V-12 Marines and were supposed to start their duty on campus, studying military-oriented subjects in preparation to become lieutenants.

The only problem for the Wisconsin football team was that the V-12 program was based at the University of Michigan. Nine Badgers from the 1942 team, including Hirsch, transferred to Michigan, where they were dubbed the "Lend-Lease Badgers."

Hirsch became the most versatile Wolverine athlete ever, the first to letter in four sports—football, basketball, track and baseball. He showed his all-around athleticism during the 1944 Big Ten Outdoor Track Championships at Illinois. He had a long jump of 22'5¾" inches during the preliminary round. He then left the track meet and after a 150-mile car trip to Bloomington, Indiana, pitched the second game of a doubleheader, tossing a four-hitter in a 12–1 win. His long-jump mark, incidentally, held up for third place.

In 1945 Hirsch tried out with the Chicago Cubs and was drafted in the first round by the Chicago Rockets of the All-America Football Conference and the Los Angeles Rams of the NFL.

He loved baseball, but Hirsch signed with the Rockets because they gave him a $7,000

deal, and he wanted to get married to Ruth Stahmer, his high school sweetheart. The couple had two children, a son, Winn, and a daughter, Patty.

In 1949, after a series of injuries that nearly ruined his career—including a fractured skull—Hirsch signed with the Rams and embarked on a record-setting career that earned him a world championship ring in 1951.

He was an amazingly popular figure in Los Angeles during his career, lunching with Charlie Chaplin and becoming friends with Richard Nixon and Ronald Reagan. Hirsch also made three movies—*Crazylegs* in 1953, *Unchained* in 1955 and *Zero Hour!* in 1957.

After his playing days, Hirsch joined the Union Oil Company as director of sports and special events. He then returned to the Rams as general manager (succeeding Pete Rozelle) and later as assistant to the team president.

But perhaps his greatest contributions to his home state came after he returned to UW as athletic director in 1969, at a time when the Athletic Department was $200,000 in debt and the football team had gone 0–19–1 over the previous two seasons.

Hirsch went around the state selling the Badgers through the sheer force of his personality. "When he was here, the toughest times, there wasn't anybody in the world that could have done a better job," Esser said.

For the Badger faithful, Hirsch was like a Pied Piper, entertaining the older ones with stories and the younger ones with magic tricks. "It didn't make any difference where you went," said Palmer "Butch" Strickler, a longtime UW booster and friend of Hirsch's. "You just walk in a place, and all the focus of attention was on him, right now."

Hirsch started a campaign to "Get the red out" and helped increase attendance at football games from an average per game of 43,000 to 70,000 in only four years. When the football team snapped a 23-game winless streak with a 23–17 victory over Iowa his first year, he joined celebrating students at campus bars.

During his tenure, the department expanded from 12 men's sports to 25 men's and women's programs. Hirsch retired in 1987 but remained active as an ambassador for the Badgers.

Hirsch was asked in an interview how he would like to have his tenure as UW athletic director remembered. "I hope people will say, 'Those were great years,'" he said.

UW retired Hirsch's No. 40, and he was also named to the school's all-time football team in 1969. He was a member of the Athletic Department/ National W Club inaugural Hall of Fame class in 1990, one of five Hall of Fames to which he belongs.

The *Crazylegs* name lives on in Madison on a popular run/walk in the spring that usually attracts more than 10,000 participants and is one of the Athletic Department's biggest fundraisers. Hirsch served as the official starter at every race, starting in 1982, then greeted all the finishers with a high-five at the 50-yard line of Camp Randall Stadium, until his death.

Elroy Hirsch

PAT RICHTER

1960–1962, end
UW athletic director, 1989–2004

It has been a charmed life. There is no other way to describe it. Pat Richter knows this better than anyone else.

Growing up in Madison; winning a state basketball title at Madison East in 1958; the last nine-time letter-winner at UW; a two-time All-American in football as a wide receiver who played in the 1963 Rose Bowl, one of college football's all-time great games; a first-round draft pick of the Washington Redskins who spent nine seasons in the NFL.

Richter can talk about meeting presidents, including John F. Kennedy, Lyndon Johnson, Gerald Ford and both Bushes. He's got countless stories about sharing a room on the road for five years with Sonny Jurgensen, playing for Vince Lombardi or chatting with Joe DiMaggio. He used to take batting practice with the Washington Senators. He once stepped into the cage after Ted Williams.

"Where does it end?" Richter said, a sense of awe in his voice, in an interview prior to his retirement as UW athletic director in 2004. "It's just unbelievable. Obviously, you've worked hard to do that. How fortunate can you be?"

Yes, Richter had plenty of good fortune in his life. But he also had terrific athletic ability, a strong work ethic and uncanny business sense.

He also never forgot his roots. First and foremost, he was a Madison guy, an East Sider, to be specific. That was a bond that was never broken.

"He came up with a value system that was based on the blue-collar neighborhoods," said Dave Kelliher, who has known Richter since high school. "He lived down in Yahara Place.

Pat was just a hard worker. He achieved an awful lot because he worked hard at everything he did.

"When you look at the bottom line with Pat Richter, I don't know that he's ever not been successful in anything he's attempted to do. That's the overriding thing."

Richter called the 1950s "a great time to grow up" in the city. Every Sunday, the neighborhood kids gathered on the fields east of the Yahara River to play whatever sport was in season. If you wanted to play with the older kids, you had to prove you belonged.

By the time Richter reached high school, he was an accomplished athlete in every sport he played.

"There wasn't anything he couldn't do," Kelliher said. "When he was in high school, he was already a man. He was something else. The one thing I remember about Pat—it didn't make any difference if it was football, basketball, baseball, golf or tennis or whatever—he had such good hands. His hand-eye coordination was something.

"You usually see bigger guys, and you think they're going to be kind of oafy. He wasn't at all."

Richter eventually grew to 6'5" and could run fairly well for someone of his size. After Richter led Madison East to the state basketball title, and scored 50 points against Cuba City in one game, Wisconsin basketball coach John Erickson, as well as other schools, suddenly became interested.

After a visit to Kansas, Richter ended up signing a letter of intent to play basketball there, remarkably without ever setting foot in Phog Allen Fieldhouse.

Pat Richter

He was eventually persuaded to go to Wisconsin by Gene Calhoun, a Madison attorney and Badger assistant baseball coach.

"That's when Gene probably gave me the best advice I ever had," Richter said. "Gene said, 'If you really want to play baseball, maybe professionally, you're better off in the Big Ten and in Madison than you are in the Big Eight in Kansas.' I decided he was probably right, and it was probably (an) impulse to go (to Kansas)."

The only thing that concerned Richter was telling Erickson he also wanted to play football. That turned out to be no problem, since Erickson was just happy to have him at Wisconsin.

On Mondays the freshman football players scrimmaged the varsity. Richter first made a name for himself when he tangled with William "Butch" Kellogg, who was one of the tougher guys on the team.

The two traded elbows, and Richter finally hauled off and took a swing, fortunately missing the single-bar facemask on Kellogg's helmet. All the varsity players started murmuring when Richter's punch knocked Kellogg down.

The next day Richter found out he broke Kellogg's nose. "Butch was kind of a grizzled guy," Richter said. "It was probably one of the better things to happen to give you a little credibility."

Richter was the consummate student-athlete and one of the most accomplished and versatile performers in school history. He lettered three times each in football, basketball and baseball.

Even though he came to Wisconsin on a basketball grant-in-aid, that turned out to be his worst sport. As it turned out, Richter really couldn't do everything. He rarely saw the court and averaged 2.7 points in 38 career games.

But he put up prodigious numbers in the other two sports, including a hefty .353 batting average, 20 home runs and 74 RBIs in baseball, in which he earned All–Big Ten honors as a first baseman.

He earned All-America distinction twice as an end in football and led the NCAA in receiving as a junior with 47 receptions for 817 yards and eight touchdowns. He earned lasting fame in the 1963 Rose Bowl, teaming with quarterback Ron Vander Kelen to lead one of the most amazing comebacks in bowl history. Trailing Southern California 42–14 after the first play of the fourth quarter, the Badgers scored 23 points in the fourth quarter only to run out of time and lose 42–37. Richter caught 11 passes for 163 yards. He became the school's seventh player elected to the College Football Hall of Fame in 1996.

Richter was also an accomplished student and earned academic All-America honors in 1962. He was Wisconsin's Big Ten Medal of Honor winner (for academic and athletic excellence) in 1963 and was inducted into the Verizon/CoSIDA (College Sports Information Directors of America) Academic All-America Hall of Fame in 1995.

Although never an all-pro, Richter had his moments in the NFL, finishing his eight-year career with 99 receptions for 1,315 yards and 14 touchdowns—including three scores in the 1968 season opener against Chicago—and ranking third in the league in punting with a 42.4-yard average in 1966.

But much like another former Badger great, Elroy Hirsch, Richter's biggest impact at Wisconsin came in his tenure as athletic director.

Donna Shalala, who was chancellor at the time, convinced Richter to leave his job as vice president for personnel at Oscar Mayer Foods Corp. in Madison in 1989 to lead an Athletic Department in the midst of a crisis. He inherited a program with a $2.1 million deficit, decaying facilities, several struggling teams and eroding fan support.

"I remember meeting with (Richter) on one of those first occasions, and he kind of said, 'What did I get myself into?'" said Minnesota athletic director Joel Maturi, who was an assistant athletic director at Wisconsin at the time.

"He's looking at our financial situation, which is being done on pencil and paper—I'm telling you the truth, it was not all computerized. For somebody who was an executive at Oscar Mayer, he knew things were in disarray, but I don't think he realized how much they were in disarray until he obviously started the job."

One of the toughest early decisions Richter had to make was the cutting of five sports— including baseball, which he loved—to help balance the budget and send the school on its way toward compliance with federal gender-equity rules.

The decade-and-a-half that followed for Wisconsin athletics was one of the most successful stretches in school history, including three Rose Bowl titles, a Final Four appearance in 2000 and more than 50 Big Ten team titles. Richter's tenure also produced more academic All–Big Ten honorees than any other school in the conference.

Richter's genius was in his hiring of coaches, especially Barry Alvarez, who turned around the football program—which was the cornerstone of the rebuilding project.

Stu Jackson, Dick Bennett and Bo Ryan were hired in succession, and each elevated the once-forlorn men's basketball program. Richter then tabbed Mike Eaves to take over a men's hockey program in decline, and it won the NCAA title in 2006.

"I think Pat's greatest strength is his ability to hire the right people, to surround himself with the right people, to put them in the right positions, give them the authority and responsibility to do their jobs and to allow them to do their jobs," Maturi said.

The health of the three revenue-generating programs allowed the athletic department to build a healthy $6.2 million reserve and fueled a facilities building boom, including the Kohl Center, University Ridge Golf Course, the Fetzer Academic Learning Center and the $109 million renovation of Camp Randall Stadium.

"If you look through the history of college athletics, I'm not sure anybody's had any bigger impact on a program than what Pat has with the leadership he's provided," longtime Penn State athletic director Tim Curley said.

Wide receivers, although not as plentiful as rushers, also have a prominent place in the football team's history.

Sometimes football players get credited with being heroes when the description does not really apply. Dave Schreiner was a true hero in every sense of the word.

Both Madison newspapers put out extra editions after Schreiner, who played with the Badgers from 1940–1942 and later became a first lieutenant for the U.S. Marine Corps, died while fighting in Okinawa in World War II. Such was the impact Schreiner had at Wisconsin.

He was a two-time All-America end and the Western Conference Most Valuable Player in 1942. He was also, by all accounts, even a finer person.

Schreiner, a member of the Sixth Marine Division, suffered fatal wounds after being shot in the upper torso while leading an assault on the last Japanese stronghold on the island. It happened 20 hours before organized resistance ended. He died the following day, June 21, 1945, at the age of 24.

He was one of two stars of the fabled 1942 team to die during the war. Fourteen days earlier, tackle Bob Baumann, also a member of the Sixth Division, was killed in action on Okinawa.

Schreiner, a right end, and Baumann, a left tackle, entered school together and became fast friends. They graduated together in 1943; they enlisted together, went through Marine training together at Parris Island, South Carolina, and Quantico, Virginia; they saw action together in the South Pacific and, tragically, both died there as well.

Henry J. McCormick of the *Wisconsin State Journal* captured the impact of Schreiner's death, when he wrote on July 1, 1945: "If there was ever a better football player at the University of Wisconsin, I never knew him. If there was a better end who ever played football any place, I never saw him. And if there was a boy who wore his honors with more modesty than Dave Schreiner, I never knew him."

Schreiner came to Wisconsin, along with his best friend, halfback Mark "Had" Hoskins, from the tiny town of Lancaster, located about 80 miles southwest of Madison. They were dubbed "the Touchdown Twins" for the Badgers during the early 1940s.

Schreiner, a husky 6'2" and 198 pounds, was big, fast, intelligent and a hard worker. He was equally dominating on defense as he was on offense. In a 7–7 tie with Notre Dame in the 1942 season-opener, newspaper accounts listed Schreiner as the biggest factor in holding the Fighting Irish to a single touchdown. He charged in to tackle the quarterback behind the line of scrimmage—there was no such thing as "sacks" in those days—to halt one Notre Dame drive that reached inside the Wisconsin 20-yard line.

Badger coach Harry Stuhldreher used to send weekly letters to former Badger players serving in the military. One week, he had Schreiner write the letter.

"I supposed that you could say that our season really got off to a successful start when we were able to tie Notre Dame," Schreiner wrote. "Everyone sort of gave us credit for winning this one, but we prefer to claim only a tie. The old scoreboard, after all, is where the results are posted and it read 7–7 when the game was over."

In a 17–7 loss to eventual national champion Ohio State, the Badgers' only loss that season, the Buckeyes' offense tested Schreiner's side of the line only twice. Ohio State liked to run sweeps to that side with Eugene Fekete. The first time it tried that, Schreiner stopped him behind the line of scrimmage.

The Buckeyes tried the same thing with Les Horvath, another member of the team's vaunted backfield. Schreiner treated him the same way, dropping him behind the line of scrimmage. According to the reports, the rest of the game Ohio State never tried to run at Schreiner again.

"When Dave Schreiner stopped 'em, they stayed stopped," the Wisconsin Sports News Service said in its account of the game.

Still, Schreiner received most of his accolades on offense. He caught 16 passes for 350 yards in 10 games that season. He was known for clutch plays throughout his career, including the winning touchdowns in games against Ohio State and Minnesota.

He had a 73-yard reception for a touchdown against Marquette, one of three he scored in a span of four-and-a-half minutes. As a senior, he played 60 minutes in each of the Ohio State, Iowa, Notre Dame and Northwestern games. He was never injured and never had to take a timeout. He was named co-captain that year, along with Hoskins.

Schreiner was a first at Wisconsin in a lot of ways, including the first two-time All-American. He was the closest thing you could find to a unanimous All-American in 1942, named to "14 or 15 national teams."

At the time, Schreiner was considered to be the greatest end in Badgers football history.

He had a chance to remain in the States after graduation and play football, but he was anxious to serve his country and requested overseas duty.

"Most of us will be in there with you boys in a short while, and the season has certainly

helped to get us in shape for the days to come," Schreiner wrote in that letter to the former Badgers in the Armed Forces.

After Schreiner's death, a statement from Stuhldreher ran in the *Grant County Independent* that said: "At Wisconsin, we called him 'Big Dave,' not because of his physique but because of his all-around makeup. His personality, modesty, unselfishness, and friendship all were big. His loss leaves a big vacuum—as big as Dave himself was in all ways—in all our lives."

Schreiner was the first Badgers player elected to the National Football Foundation College Hall of Fame in 1955. His No. 80 was retired, and he was selected by fans to the school's All-Time Team.

* * *

Barry Alvarez used to take all kinds of grief during his coaching tenure about his teams' struggles in the passing game. That was especially true when Mike Samuel was the quarterback for the 1998 team that went to the Rose Bowl. Even Alvarez used to joke about some of Samuel's passes, saying they looked like they were coming out of his hand "sideways."

So, there were more than a few people around the Big Ten who were shocked during the 2003 season when the Badger Lee Evans became the Big Ten's career leader in receiving yards with 3,468 yards.

The Badgers actually started opening up their offense a few years earlier, going to more formations with three and four receivers that were so common at other schools.

Part of it was to take advantage of Evans, who Alvarez called the best receiver he ever coached. "I don't know if I've ever been around anyone who has stronger hands than he does," Alvarez said. "Then the next thing that he does, besides having the speed and being able to run routes and cut things off sharply and be physical, is his transition from once he catches the ball and being able to accelerate and turn into a runner."

Evans had a phenomenal junior season in 2001 when he caught 75 passes for a Big Ten single-season record 1,545 yards and was a finalist for the Biletnikoff Award given to the nation's top receiver. After making the decision to return for his senior year, he looked even better during practice the following spring.

To be safe, Alvarez planned to use Evans for only a handful of plays in the annual spring game, but it turned out to be one too many. Evans suffered a torn anterior cruciate ligament in his left knee after landing awkwardly on the turf at Camp Randall Stadium while trying to catch a deep pass.

After surgery in May, he pushed himself incredibly hard to try to make it back for the start of the Big Ten Conference season. He went through some drills in fall camp and appeared to be on track, but each week, he failed to get medical clearance from the doctors. Finally, in early November, he learned he needed a second reconstructive surgery.

With his draft hopes squashed, he made the decision to come back in 2003 for his final year of eligibility. He had another huge season, catching 64 passes for 1,213 yards, and by the time he left, he held almost every school receiving record, including receptions (175) and receiving touchdowns (27) in addition to his Big Ten record for receiving yards.

He was drafted in the first round by the Buffalo Bills and made a quick impact as a rookie in 2004, catching 48 passes for 843 yards and nine touchdowns.

Most of the records Evans broke belonged to Al Toon (1982–1984), who had eclipsed many of the marks set by Richter.

There may have never been a more physically gifted receiver to pass through Madison than Toon, who also had interests in martial arts and ballet and was graceful enough that he was invited to try out for the American Ballet Theatre in New York.

He had ideal size at 6'4", to go with blazing speed and the athleticism to set the UW record in the triple jump at 53'7¼", which still stood more than 20 years later.

In football, Toon set UW career records at the time for receptions (131), yardage (2,103) and receiving touchdowns (19), in addition to single-season records for catches (54 in 1984), yardage (881 in 1983) and receiving touchdowns (nine in 1983). Not bad for somebody who played in a run-oriented offense.

He was so popular among Badgers fans, cries of "Tooooooon!" usually filled Camp Randall Stadium when he caught a pass.

It was in the NFL, after being a first-round pick of the New York Jets in 1985, that Toon's potential was fully realized. He was not only one of the best wide receivers of his time, but of any time. He had more catches (355) in his first five NFL seasons than San Francisco 49er Jerry Rice (346).

He was selected to play in three Pro Bowls and was voted the most valuable player on the Jets three times, something only Hall of Fame quarterback Joe Namath had done.

But on November 27, 1992, five months before his 30th birthday, Toon retired after eight seasons, with more than 500 receptions and 6,000 yards, walking away from a million-dollar salary.

He really didn't have much choice. On November 8, 1992, he sustained what he estimated was the fifth concussion of his pro career, when his helmet glanced off that of Denver linebacker Michael Brooks. Subsequent neurological tests showed Toon, who suffered from post-concussion symptoms, had reached a point of imminent danger.

"I didn't necessarily make the decision (to retire)," he said. "The doctors made the decision; I just agreed with them."

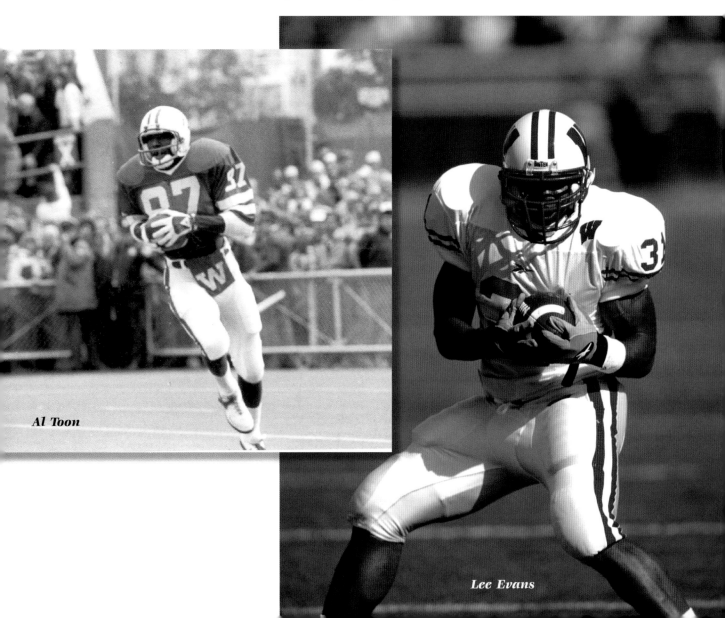

Al Toon

Lee Evans

Even with the Badgers' steady stream of 1,000-yard rushers, it was the receivers who went on to have some of the best success in the NFL. That was evident when Chris Chambers made the Pro Bowl with the Miami Dolphins in 2005.

Chambers came from Bedford (Ohio) High School, where he was two years ahead of Evans. Not only were the two prep teammates, but it was also Chambers who paved the way and set an example for Evans to follow. The other common thread between the two was wide receivers coach Henry Mason, who recruited both players and convinced them they could flourish at Wisconsin, despite the run-first offense.

"He's an outstanding recruiter," Evans said. "He was just really down to earth. He knows how to deal with people, from my family to my coaches, he met my girlfriend at the time, everything. He really knows how to make you feel comfortable."

Mason was hired by Barry Alvarez in 1995 to replace Jay Norvell, and between 1998–2006, the Badgers had six receivers drafted into the NFL, including three in the first two rounds— Tony Simmons (second round in 1998), Chambers (second round in 2001) and Evans (first round in 2004). Also drafted were Donald Hayes (fourth round in 1998), Brandon Williams (third round in 2006) and Jonathan Orr (sixth round in 2006), while Ahmad Merritt made it as a free agent.

Of the top nine players in career receiving yards at Wisconsin, going into the 2007 season, six were coached by Mason in just 12 years at the school.

"His coaching style is definitely unique," Evans said. "He can really get under your skin sometimes. At first, when you're not really used to it, you're going out there trying to do things to shut him up, to prove him wrong. But the more you do it, you realize, 'I can do it. He's just trying to get me to that point, any way he can do it.'"

* * *

After Pat Richter, tight end Stu Voigt might have been one of Wisconsin's best all-around athletes. Voigt won eight letters during his UW career, three each in football and track and two in baseball, one short of Richter. Voigt would have had a ninth, but he had to report for football one spring and missed the baseball season.

A former Madison West athlete, Voigt spent his sophomore year as a tailback and tight end. He was a wingback as a junior and the team's fourth-leading ball carrier and second-leading receiver, before finding a home at tight end as a senior in 1969. That season he caught 39 passes for 439 yards, setting a Badgers single-season record at the time for a tight end.

He also hit .350 during two years on the varsity in baseball and was a standout in track who once set a national high school shot put record of more than 67 feet. Voigt went on to an 11-year NFL career with the Minnesota Vikings, playing in three Super Bowls, with an overall record of 108–50–2. He was named to the Vikings' all-time team by fans in 1985, and when he finished his career he was the Vikings' all-time leader in yardage, receptions and touchdowns.

The Defensive Linemen

Tim Krumrie had modest goals when he arrived at Wisconsin in 1979, saying he "just wanted to make the squad" as a freshman. Krumrie was recruited as a linebacker out of Mondovi, Wisconsin, and had never played as a down lineman.

But after starter Danny Yourg suffered a dislocated elbow, Krumrie was switched to nose guard eight days before the opener against Purdue. Over the next four years, Krumrie started 46 consecutive games. He missed only four or five plays during the Ohio State game as a freshman. Other than that, he played every down on defense for four years.

"You just have to keep going all the time," Krumrie said. "It's when you let up that you get hurt."

There was never any danger of letting up with Krumrie. While there have been many defensive players at Wisconsin with more talent, few could match Krumrie for consistency, durability and effort.

Former Badgers center Ron Versnik had the task of trying to block Krumrie in practice. "Tim really makes you work," Versnik said. "It sure would be a job facing him on Saturdays. Some guys you can hit, and they'll either give up or fall down. Not Tim. He's got such good

Tim Krumrie

balance, and he's so aggressive that he just keeps going and gets to the play."

As a freshman, Krumrie never really felt comfortable and got by on sheer effort. The next three years, he was a first-team All–Big Ten selection.

He had a huge junior season in 1981, when he led the team with 135 tackles and was a key figure in the Badgers' 7–5 finish, earning Associated Press All-America first-team honors. It started in the opening game against Michigan, when Krumrie helped ignite a 21–14 upset with 13 tackles, earning national player-of-the-week recognition.

"If you block him and knock him down, that's not good enough because he will get up and run the play down from behind," Michigan All-America guard Kurt Becker said after the game.

Nose guards were not supposed to make that many tackles, but when Krumrie left, he was the school's career leader with 444 stops and still ranked third going into the 2007 season. He also still held the school record for solo tackles with 276.

Despite his extremely productive college career, Krumrie was not drafted until the 10th round by the Cincinnati Bengals in 1983. "I was too short, too slow and too light," Krumrie said. "I was about 240 and ran a 5-flat 40 when I reported, but a computer can't measure your heart or your desire."

He used that draft snub to stoke the fire inside of him to burn even hotter. He started 95 straight games in the NFL, making it 178 straight since his high school days, and was named to the 1988 and 1989 Pro Bowls, while leading the Bengals in tackles for four straight years.

Unfortunately, he broke the fibula and tibia in his left leg while tackling San Francisco 49er running back Roger Craig in the first quarter of the 1989 Super Bowl. He returned to play with the Bengals through 1994 and eventually became an NFL coach.

Don Voss, 6'3", 185 pounds, from Milwaukee, could have been one of the best defensive players in school history. Freshmen were eligible to play due to the Korean War, and in 1951 he was brought up from the junior varsity and filled a big void after an injury to Gene Felker.

Voss soon became a mainstay of the "Hard Rocks" defense that ranked first nationally in total defense, allowing 154.8 yards per game, and scoring defense, allowing 6.6 points per game. He twice blocked and recovered punts to help win games. As a sophomore, he was the youngest player on the National Football Writers Association (*Look*) All-America Team at age 19, after previously earning All-America recognition in track. He continued his impressive play early in the Rose Bowl against Southern California, before suffering a knee injury in the second quarter that ended his career.

The "Hard Rocks" had plenty of other standouts, including All-America end Pat O'Donahue, who spent one season with the San Francisco 49ers and one with the Packers.

The next great era for Wisconsin defensive linemen started in the mid-1990s with Tarek Saleh, who came to the school from Woodbridge, Connecticut, as a highly regarded linebacker prospect, spurning Penn State for the Badgers.

He was regarded as a "tweener," an undersized defensive end (6'2", 243) who overcame his lack of size by being one of the most intense Badger players of his time.

Tarek Saleh

Wendell Bryant

One of his finest moments came in a 17–9 victory against Penn State in 1995, when he had three sacks, disrupted reverses and generally chased down ball carriers all over the field, causing Penn State football coach Joe Paterno to say, "That was as good as anybody's played against us that I can remember."

Saleh was an All-American in 1996 and left school as the career leader in tackles for loss (58) and sacks (33), records that remained 10 years later.

If there was anyone who came close to matching Saleh's non-stop motor, it was another undersized defensive end, Tom Burke (6'4", 250), from tiny Poplar, Wisconsin, who came within one of reaching Saleh's career sacks record.

Tom Burke

Burke had terrific speed and played the game with an almost maniacal passion that made him a dominating force as a senior on the 1998 Rose Bowl championship team. He led the nation and set a Big Ten record with 22 sacks for minus-130 yards and finished with a school-record 31 tackles for loss while being named a consensus All-American.

"I had a lot of people telling me, 'You ain't gonna play, you ain't gonna have a chance to do anything. You'll never play there,'" Burke said. "And that's one of the reasons why I came to Wisconsin."

Burke had five tackles for loss and four sacks in UW's 24–3 win over Penn State, which clinched the Rose Bowl trip. Earlier, he had three sacks and five tackles for loss in a 31–0 victory over Iowa.

During the week before the Rose Bowl, UCLA coach Bob Toledo made the mistake of referring to Burke as "Tom Barnes," the name of a former quarterback of his at Pacific in the early 1980s. It was just one more slight heaped on the Badgers and Burke in their season-long search for respect. Burke had a sack and was a constant thorn in UCLA's side in the Badgers' 38–31 victory.

"Tom Burke's a great football player, and obviously I slipped when I called him 'Barnes' in our meeting," Toledo admitted later. "So, I went up to him the other day and said, 'Hey, Tom, I'm really sorry.' And he says, 'Coach Rodgers, don't worry about a thing.' I love his personality and I love watching him play."

Defensive tackle Wendell Bryant also burst on the scene as a true freshman in that game, with a sack of UCLA quarterback Cade McNown on fourth-and-three to seal the victory. The next three years, Big Ten offensive linemen struggled to block Bryant, who finished his career ranked fifth in UW history with 24 sacks. Bryant was a 2001 All-American and the 12th pick overall in the 2002 NFL draft by the Arizona Cardinals.

Defensive end Erasmus James thought his career was over after suffering a dislocated hip during fall camp in 2003. Only after sitting out the season and consulting a specialist on the East Coast did the condition improve enough to allow James to return as a senior in 2004.

A late bloomer who played only one year of high school football and was discovered by Wisconsin coaches at a Florida high school all-star game late in the recruiting process, James was in the midst of a Burke-type season before suffering a high ankle sprain on a cut block against Purdue. That caused him to miss the equivalent of two full games and hampered his effectiveness when he did return for the final two regular-season games.

Still, James led the team with eight sacks and was so disruptive when healthy that he was named the Big Ten Defensive Player of the Year and a finalist for the Nagurski, Bednarik, Lombardi and Hendricks awards. He was also named the Big Ten's Defensive Lineman of the Year, an award won four times in seven years by the Badgers, including Burke, Bryant (twice) and James.

When a reporter tried to compare James to former Illinois standout Simeon Rice, the Big Ten's career sacks leader with 44.5, Wisconsin coach Barry Alvarez balked.

"To say (James) is as dominating as Simeon Rice is an injustice to 'Ras,' because he's much, much more physical than Simeon Rice ever was, or probably is today," Alvarez said.

Even some of the darkest days in Wisconsin football history could not dim the beacon that was Troy Vincent's career. In his first three years, the Badgers had a 4–29 record. Vincent toiled in near anonymity, seldom seen on national television and rarely playing in significant games.

He was a rare athlete—think Deion Sanders, without the self-promotion—the kind of talent that seldom found its way to Madison at that time. Vincent, from Trenton, New Jersey, grew up playing basketball and played one year of football at Pennsbury High School.

His recruiting visits were to Syracuse, Clemson, Rutgers, North Carolina and Wisconsin. His mother, Alma, took just one trip with her son and fell in love with UW, thinking it was a great institution in a beautiful place.

"I came here to get an education," Vincent told the Wisconsin State Journal prior to his final game in 1991. "Football is secondary to me. I might be a pretty good football player, but I chose this university to get a decent education. I'm a better student than I am a football player. I work hard in the classroom. I've achieved a lot, that a lot of people didn't think I'd accomplish."

His education on the field was a lesson in perseverance. He was a three-year starter but struggled at first with the new defense after Barry Alvarez arrived in 1990. However, in the second half of the season, he was a terror: 11 tackles and an interception against Ohio State; 10 tackles against Illinois; two touchdown saves at Northwestern; defensive player of the game against Indiana; and a 71-yard punt return for a touchdown at Michigan State.

That led to sky-high expectations going into his senior year. In the opener against Western Illinois, the Badgers fell in an early 13–0 hole. Vincent returned four punts for 146 yards, including one for a school-record 90 yards. He returned two kickoffs for 95 yards and set up three scores to spark the Badgers to a 31–13 victory.

As a senior, he drew the opponent's best receiver in man coverage each week and tied a school record by breaking up 15 passes. He was usually left alone on the wide side of the field and asked to take away that part of the field from the offense.

He was named the Big Ten co-Defensive Player of the Year and was runner-up for the Thorpe Award, given to the nation's best defensive back.

"He's hardly ever been on TV, but he's gained the respect of everybody in the whole Big Ten area," Alvarez said that season. "Anybody who's studied our films knows he's a legitimate All-American. That's not just hype or press. This is a kid who's gone out and done it."

The NFL scouts showed up in droves, and Vincent was a first-round pick, the seventh overall, by the Miami Dolphins in the 1992 draft. He played four seasons in Miami before signing as a free agent with the Philadelphia Eagles in 1996. He was a four-time All-Pro who led the NFL in interceptions in 1999 and registered a career-best 82 tackles the same season.

As accomplished as Vincent was on the field, he did even more off it. He was named the 2002 Walter Payton NFL Man of the Year, which recognizes off-field contributions and football excellence.

In March 2003, he pledged $250,000 to endow a scholarship at Wisconsin for future defensive backs and another $100,000 toward the renovation of Camp Randall Stadium. The

Wisconsin football office reception area is named in his honor.

His explanation for wanting to give back was simple and elegant. "Much is given, much is required," Vincent said. "The University of Wisconsin gave me an opportunity to receive a first-class education and prepared me for the National Football League. Much is given, much is required."

While Vincent fell just short of the Thorpe Award, Jamar Fletcher became the first Wisconsin player to win it as a junior in 2000, when he was also chosen

Troy Vincent

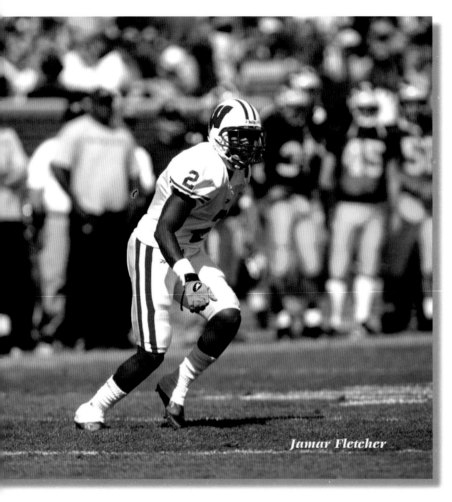

Jamar Fletcher

in only 20 games in his first two seasons.

The bigger the game, the better Fletcher played. He returned an interception 46 yards for a touchdown in the fourth quarter as a redshirt freshman in the 1999 Rose Bowl, the final points in the Badgers' 38–31 victory.

He liked to talk almost as much as he liked to play. As a sophomore, he told reporters he wanted to cover Michigan State star Plaxico Burress all over the field, and if the coaches didn't agree, he would demand it. Fletcher got his wish and was matched up with the Big Ten's best receiver in single coverage all day. Burress finished with five catches for 53 yards, and Fletcher intercepted two passes as UW upset the 11th-ranked Spartans 40–10.

Fletcher was suspended by the NCAA for three games at the start of the 2000 season—one of 27 players to receive suspensions of one or three games—for receiving unadvertised discounts from an area shoe store. The suspensions had to be served in the first four games. Fletcher talked the coaches into letting him play in the second game against quarterback Joey Harrington and Oregon's prolific passing attack.

He turned in one of his best games, grabbing three interceptions, giving him 17 in 21 career games. He also played three snaps at wideout, dropping the only pass thrown to him, to become the first UW player since Kevin Huntley in 1996 to play offense and defense in the same game.

as an All-American and Big Ten Defensive Player of the Year.

A speedy, elusive option quarterback at Hazelwood East High School in St. Louis, Fletcher developed a taste for the end zone, once scoring five touchdowns in a playoff victory.

Even though he moved to defense at Wisconsin, he kept it up. Every time he intercepted a pass, something he did with remarkable consistency, Fletcher looked to score. He set a Big Ten career record with five interceptions returned for touchdowns

"(Fletcher) really wanted to play," Wisconsin coach Barry Alvarez said of his All-America defensive back. "He didn't want to sit for three straight weeks. We felt it was the time to go let him play."

Despite missing the three games, he still finished the season with seven interceptions, setting school career records with 21 interceptions and 459 interception return yards in 32 career games.

He left for the NFL after his junior year, becoming one of four players in the Alvarez era to jump to the NFL with eligibility remaining, along with running backs Michael Bennett and Brian Calhoun and receiver Lee DeRamus.

After Fletcher, the Badgers figured to wait for some time to uncover another ballhawking defensive back of that caliber. It took only two years.

Jim Leonhard was a walk-on from tiny Tony, Wisconsin, a three-sport prep legend in the northwest part of the state who was discovered after running the 40-yard dash in 4.4 seconds at a Wisconsin summer football camp. Alvarez refused to believe the initial clocking and had Leonhard run it again. Then again. All three times were 4.4.

At 5'8" and 175 pounds, Leonhard's only scholarship offer was to play football and baseball at Division II Minnesota-Duluth. He elected to walk on at Wisconsin, where he became one of the most endearing stories of recent years.

Leonhard contributed on special teams as a true freshman, then became a two-time, first-team All-American and three-time, first-team All–Big Ten selection at safety. Showing an incredible nose for the football, Leonhard became the first sophomore to be named the team's MVP since 1947 after setting team

Jim Leonhard

Jason Doering

records for interceptions (11) and punt return yards (434).

His senior season, teams stopped throwing his way, and Leonhard had only one interception going into the final regular-season game at Iowa. He picked off two passes to tie Fletcher for the school record with 21. Leonhard also set school records for career punt return yards (1,347) and average (12.8) and broke his own single-season record for punt return yards with 470 in 2003.

At a school noted for successful walk-ons like safety Jason Doering and offensive tackles Joe Panos and Mark Tauscher, who all went on to NFL careers, Leonhard's accomplishments topped them all. He became the school's ultimate walk-on success story.

"They're all great stories if you take a look at them separately," Leonhard said. "When you combine them, the main thing you look at is Coach Alvarez. He has given walk-ons a chance, and they've proven there are guys that fall through the cracks, and if you give them a chance they can do great things for you."

Another walk-on from the state who became an All-America safety in 1981 was Matt VandenBoom from Kimberly. He ignited the 21–14 victory over top-ranked Michigan in the opener that season by intercepting three passes. The 6'4" VandenBoom was named first-team All–Big Ten in 1981 and 1982, although his senior season was the start of a concussion problem that ended his NFL career.

He collapsed on the field in the 1982 season opener after getting kicked in the head.

He spent three weeks on the sidelines before getting clearance to play again, although the drowsiness and blurred vision stayed with him throughout the season. He suffered another major concussion during a preseason scrimmage with the Buffalo Bills the following summer and elected to retire. It wasn't a hard decision to make. In 1979 VandenBoom's freshman teammate, safety Jay Seiler, died from a head injury suffered during spring drills.

Perhaps the first great defensive back for the Badgers was Ed Withers, from Madison Central High School, who became the first African American at the school to earn All-America recognition, in 1950 and 1951. In a game at Iowa in 1950, he intercepted three passes for 103 yards. He finished his career with eight interceptions.

Wisconsin's best cornerbacks in the 1980s were Richard Johnson and Nate Odomes. Johnson was as adept at blocking kicks as he was at covering receivers. He had nine blocked kicks in his career, including six in 1984. While being named an All-American that year, he also had three interceptions and seven passes defended. He was a first-round pick of the Houston Oilers, No. 11 overall, and played with them from 1985 to 1992.

Odomes was a first-team All–Big Ten pick in 1986, when he intercepted seven passes. He was a second-round NFL draft pick by the Buffalo Bills the following year and made the Pro Bowl in 1992 and 1993.

Linebackers

Wisconsin, surprisingly, has never had a first-team All-American linebacker. Hal Faverty is listed as a defensive end in school records, although he also played linebacker when he was honored in 1951 as a member of the "Hard Rocks" defense.

Still, the Badgers have a lengthy list of excellent players at the position.

Rick Graf and Tim Jordan played against each other in high school. Graf was from Madison Memorial and Jordan was from Madison La Follette. It was hard to think of one without the other. Together, they became known as "Thunder" and "Lightning," respectively.

"In Rick Graf and Tim Jordan, we have a little something special," UW coach Dave

Tim Jordan

McClain said. "They are fine athletes who are capable of making that big play when you need it, and their athletic abilities enable us to do some different things on defense."

Graf was a four-year starter at outside linebacker who returned from knee surgery to start all 12 games in 1986, when he was named second-team All–Big Ten. Jordan was a three-year starter at the other outside linebacker spot who had impressive speed, running the 40-yard dash in 4.5 seconds. "We never had speed like that on the outside before," McClain said.

When they were sophomores in 1984, the Badgers ranked second in the Big Ten in total defense, scoring defense and pass defense. Jordan finished his career with a then-record 27 sacks and set the current Big Ten single-game record with six against Northwestern in 1985. He was a fourth-round draft pick of the New England Patriots, although his NFL career was cut short by injury. Graf was picked in the second round of the same draft by the Miami Dolphins and went on to play seven years for three teams.

Coach Barry Alvarez, a former linebacker and linebackers coach, once called Pete Monty, "the best linebacker I've ever been around, and I've been around a few."

Monty set the school career record for tackles with 451 and had 178 tackles, the second-best single-season in school history, while making first-team All–Big Ten as a senior in 1996.

Nick Greisen was a two-time first-team All–Big Ten choice in 2000 and 2001 and a fifth-round NFL draft pick who went on to a successful NFL career.

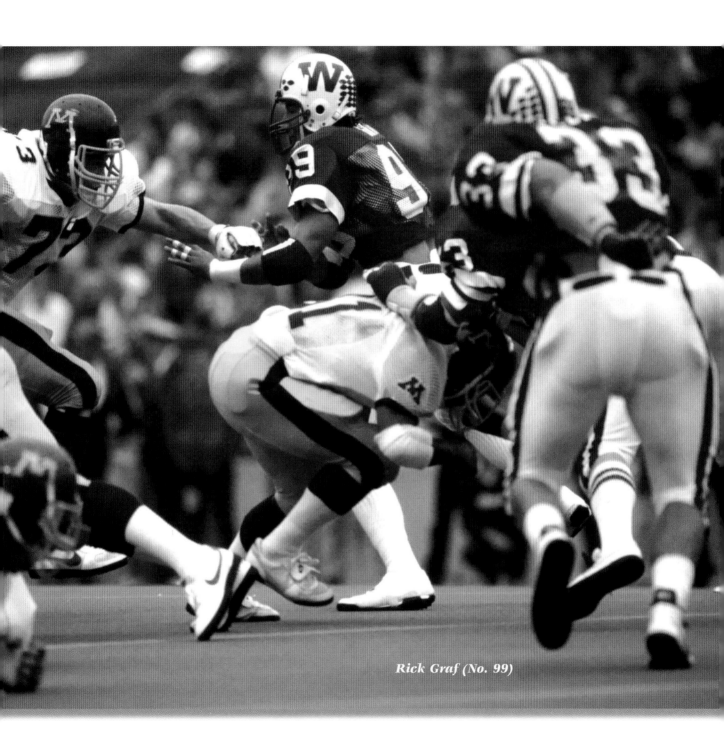

Rick Graf (No. 99)

Specialists

Pat O'Dea was once described as a football player born a generation too soon. He had everything that goes into a modern sports idol, including athletic ability, personality and a colorful nickname as the "Kangaroo Kicker."

He was 6'1½", 175 pounds, with a long, lean frame and "the finest pair of legs a man ever wore," according to one newspaper account.

His older brother was a crew coach and football trainer at Wisconsin, so Pat left his home in Melbourne, Australia and entered UW law school in 1896.

O'Dea played rugby and soccer in Australia and knew nothing of American football. As legend has it, he was watching a football practice when a ball rolled to him. He booted it back and the ball went about 60 yards, while the players on the field howled.

In his first year he got in the second half of a practice game and had an 85-yard punt but suffered a broken arm in the next game.

By 1897 he had begun to figure the game out and reportedly punted the ball against Minnesota from "goal to goal," a distance of 110 yards in those days.

In 1898–1899, O'Dea was Wisconsin's fullback, captain and field general. Sideline coaching was unheard of in those days and plays were called by captains. He was also one of the greatest drop kick specialists in football history. He had a 62-yard drop kick against Northwestern on November 15, 1898, reportedly in blizzard conditions, from near the sideline, a record that stood for 20 years.

It was said that there was "nothing Pat could not do with a football." He supposedly averaged about 50 yards per punt, held all the drop-kicking records and was equally adept as a place-kicker. He garnered nationwide fame at a time when athletes—especially football players—received much less attention.

He was Wisconsin's first football star and one of seven former Badgers players to receive college football's highest honor when he was inducted into the National Football Foundation Hall of Fame in 1962.

Jim Bakken was a good-enough athlete, after being a prep standout at Madison West, to alternate at quarterback with Dale Hackbart for a while. But Bakken made a name for himself as a kicker and punter, leading the Big Ten in punting in 1960 and 1961. He went on to become one of the most successful kickers in NFL history with the St. Louis Cardinals, a four-time Pro Bowl selection who was named to both the NFL 1960s and 1970s All-Decade teams in a 17-year career. He also went on to serve as an administrator in the UW athletic department before retiring in 2003.

While coach Barry Alvarez was not a big fan of punters and kickers, he made an exception for punter Kevin Stemke. That was probably because Stemke was regarded as more of an all-around athlete than just a punter.

Stemke was a prolific punter, winning the inaugural Ray Guy Award, presented by Guy himself, as the nation's top punter in 2000, when he averaged a school-record 44.5 yards. He set the school record for career average at 43.5 yards and had the top three season averages in school history when he departed.

Following a 13–10 loss to Michigan in 2000, Wolverines coach Lloyd Carr was so impressed with Stemke's overall contributions, he offered this unsolicited evaluation: "The thing that stood out in my mind was the play of Stemke. He's always been an outstanding punter. I think he's the best punter I've ever seen. He is a guy who has a tremendous impact on the game."

Kevin Stemke

It might be hard for contemporary fans to remember, but during stretches in the 1950s and early 1960s, Wisconsin was on the cutting edge of passing attacks in the country.

John Coatta was the first Big Ten quarterback to throw for more than 1,000 yards, finishing with 1,154, while completing 64 percent of his passes, in 1951. He also led the conference in passing the year before with 610 yards.

It was a golden age for Badger quarterbacks. Jim Haluska followed Coatta in 1952 and led the Badgers to their first Rose Bowl as a sophomore. When Haluska broke a leg playing baseball the next summer, another sophomore, Jim Miller, took over the reins in 1953. Although known more as a runner, Miller led the Big Ten in passing with 683 yards, "and they said I couldn't pass," he said later.

Dale Hackbart was one of the more colorful quarterbacks—and players—in school history, a character on and off the field. He set a school record as a junior in 1958 by intercepting seven passes, then led the Big Ten in total offense as a senior while leading the Badgers to the Rose Bowl. He attended Madison East and grew up idolizing Mickey Mantle. He hit over .300 as a senior, which led to a minor league contract with the Pittsburgh Pirates. After getting drafted in the fifth round by the Green Bay Packers in 1960, he was reportedly told by coach Vince Lombardi that "baseball players were wimps and football players were real men." Hackbart went on to a 14-year NFL career as a defensive back and linebacker.

All of that set the stage for the passing exploits in 1962 of Ron Vander Kelen.

He played just 90 seconds of college football before his senior year. While Vander Kelen missed the 1960 and 1961 seasons due to a knee injury and ineligibility, Ron Miller broke numerous school records, throwing for 2,838 yards and 19 touchdowns. Vander Kelen was one of seven candidates for the quarterback job the following year but earned the job and led Wisconsin to an early 17–8 victory over Notre Dame. "Vandy's the boy I'm going with from now on," coach Milt Bruhn told the *Wisconsin State Journal* after the game. "He and (Pat) Richter are going to be my offense."

Few football players ever enjoyed a year like Vander Kelen experienced in 1962. He led the Badgers to the Big Ten Conference championship and was named the conference's Most Valuable Player. He turned in a legendary performance in the Rose Bowl, setting Rose Bowl records with 401 passing yards, 33 completions and 48 attempts, in the 42–37 loss to Southern California. He capped his college career by winning the MVP award in the Chicago College All-Star game where he and Richter teamed up on a 73-yard scoring pass that beat the Green Bay Packers, 20–17.

Vander Kelen told the *State Journal* in 1993 that he never thought about what might have happened had he played three years at Wisconsin. "You never know," he said. "I can't imagine things could be any better. It was a dream come true.

"A lot of people claim the (Rose Bowl) game made a career for me. It was an exciting time in my life. In one year I accomplished everything you can imagine. I had an action-packed agenda. I was real fortunate so many good things happened to me."

Wisconsin's quarterback tradition took a bit of a hit after Vander Kelen left, with a couple of notable exceptions. Randy Wright started in 1982 and 1983, posting two of the top three individual passing seasons in school history and leading the Badgers to their first-ever bowl victory, 14–3 over Kansas State in the 1982 Independence Bowl. Wright set career records with 5,003 passing yards and 38 touchdowns and played five seasons in the NFL with the Packers.

He was later eclipsed by Darrell Bevell, a four-year starter who arrived on campus in 1992 from a two-year Mormon mission. He was a 25-year-old senior in 1995 who finished with 7,686 passing yards and 59 TDs in his career. But Bevell's highlight came with his legs, an unlikely 21-yard scramble around left end for the winning touchdown in the Badgers' first Rose Bowl victory, 21–16, over UCLA in 1994.

Darrell Bevell

The Coaches

It has taken the leadership of great men to produce the legacy and tradition that embody Wisconsin football. One Badger coach in particular stands among the greats the game has produced.

BARRY ALVAREZ
1990–2005
118–73–4
Big Ten titles in 1993, 1998 and 1999
Rose Bowl titles in 1994, 1999 and 2000

He warned everybody it would happen.

At his introductory press conference on January 2, 1990, Wisconsin football coach Barry Alvarez issued one of the boldest statements possible for a new coach taking over a downtrodden program.

"People need to be patient," Alvarez said. "They have to understand this is not going to turn over overnight. But let me say this: they better get season tickets now because before too long, they probably won't be able to."

It was vintage Alvarez, equal parts brashness and confidence. It was also exactly what fans needed to hear after the despair brought on by the previous three years under Don Morton. The program bottomed out in Morton's final game the year before, when an announced crowd of 29,776 showed up to watch Michigan State hammer the Badgers 31–3.

Alvarez was flush with success, coming off an incredibly successful three-year run at Notre Dame under Lou Holtz, including 23 consecutive wins in 1988 and 1989. After serving as linebackers coach in 1987, Alvarez was promoted to defensive coordinator in 1988, when the Fighting Irish went undefeated and won the national title. He was promoted to assistant head coach the following year, when Notre Dame was 12–1 and finished No. 2.

He also knew the lay of the land in the Big Ten, having served as an assistant coach at Iowa under Hayden Fry for eight seasons, from 1979 to 1986. The Hawkeyes won two Big Ten titles and went to two Rose Bowls during that stretch.

It was clear Alvarez had a plan. He told friends he wanted to be a college head coach by the age of 42. He was introduced as Badger head coach three days after his 42nd birthday.

From the first meeting with his players, it was evident a new sheriff was in town. Most of the players were home during winter break when Alvarez was hired, so there was a mixture of excitement, anticipation and trepidation when players gathered for the first team meeting inside the McClain Athletic Center.

Alvarez walked into the lecture hall followed by his assistant coaches. "It was all business," said Greg Thomas, a senior safety on the team that year. "He didn't even exchange pleasantries, didn't say hello. He just said, 'Sit up straight, feet on the floor, take your hats off. My name's Barry Alvarez and I'm the new football coach.'

"It was, 'OK, here we go.' This is what we needed, this is what we wanted, this is what was missing, some direction, some leadership, some guidance. At that point, I wouldn't say we were desperate, but we were beaten down about as low as a program could be. We were hungry and had an appetite for anything that could at least give us a chance to have some success."

But not even Alvarez envisioned what was to come—winning three Rose Bowl titles at a place where nobody else had managed to win even one. "I think it would have probably been a ridiculous goal," Alvarez said prior to the 2000 Rose Bowl. "I was just so darn busy trying to recruit guys and trying to patch (things) up. Hayden Fry used to say, 'Plowing up snakes and killing them.' I really didn't think about 10 years down the road, didn't have the opportunity. There was just too much going on."

When he arrived, Alvarez had the total support of athletic director Pat Richter and chancellor Donna Shalala. He also hired a terrific staff filled with young, aggressive recruiters like Dan McCarney, Bill Callahan, Brad Childress and Kevin Cosgrove. "Those guys could recruit," Alvarez said.

Alvarez knew the only way to contend for titles and get to the Rose Bowl was to find a way to beat Michigan and Ohio State. Given the recruiting advantages those programs enjoy in their talent-rich home states, it was obvious to Alvarez what kind of teams he needed to build.

"One thing that we felt we could get were big linemen," Alvarez said. "We could get physical linebackers. So, let's try to build a program that plays a physical brand of football and will give us a chance to beat the top teams in this league. If we can beat them, we should be able to beat the rest of the guys and win a championship."

Alvarez also set out to change the culture of losing that had enveloped the program for most of three decades. The veteran players who didn't quickly get on board were shown the door.

"We had a very intense offseason program, and that was by design," said Don Davey, a senior defensive end in Alvarez's first year. "Barry came in and he wanted to weed out the guys that weren't going to bust their tail for him and be committed to the program. Quite honestly, we had some guys on the team at that time who weren't committed to the program.

"They had a scholarship and they were kind of just along for the ride. He weeded those guys out. Some of those guys were very talented guys; they just weren't a very good fit for what he was trying to get done."

The coaching staff beat the bushes for recruits, with nothing to sell, as Alvarez liked to say, "but the blue sky." The first recruiting class, cobbled together in one month, included players like offensive lineman Joe Panos and nose tackle Lamark Shackerford, who became the heart of the first Rose Bowl team.

The formula worked as the Badgers shocked nearly everybody by defeating UCLA 21–16 in the 1994 Rose Bowl. While that game secured Alvarez's legacy, it was not enough for him.

After landing a once-in-a-lifetime recruit in tailback Ron Dayne in 1996, Alvarez surrounded him with enough talent to make Wisconsin the first Big Ten school to win back-to-back Rose Bowls following the 1998 and 1999 seasons.

But even that was not enough. It turned out Alvarez had a master plan, one he shared with McCarney, his first defensive coordinator. McCarney thought enough of Alvarez to leave the comfort and security of his assistant's job at Iowa to come to Madison.

"He told me when he took the job, when I went up there with him and left Iowa City after 36 years, he said, 'I want to turn this into

another Nebraska, where we're winning, we're going to bowl games, we're challenging for championships, we're packing the stadium,'" said McCarney.

And then the kicker.

"'Some day I want to be athletic director and name my own successor,'" McCarney quoted Alvarez as saying. "That is exactly what has happened."

Alvarez was named athletic director in April 2004, succeeding Richter and becoming one of only two people at the time at the Division I-A level to serve as head football coach and athletic director. Alvarez was simply following the career path of Bob Devaney, his former football coach at Nebraska, who also became an athletic director.

Then, at a surprise news conference on July 28, 2005, Alvarez announced the upcoming season, his 16th with the Badgers, would be his last, thus ending one of the great reclamation projects in Big Ten history. He also named defensive coordinator Bret Bielema as his hand-picked successor.

Alvarez's legacy could be measured in many ways beyond the three Rose Bowl titles and a final record of 118–73–4. Football was the economic engine that drove a revival of the entire athletic department, going from a multi-million-dollar deficit when Alvarez arrived to a $20 million reserve in 2006. Since the first Rose Bowl title, UW built the Kohl Center arena for its men's and women's basketball and hockey teams, as well as a boathouse, academic center and softball diamond, in addition to spending $109 million to renovate the football stadium.

IVAN B. WILLIAMSON
1949–1955
41–19–4
Big Ten title in 1952
Rose Bowl in 1953

Before the arrival of Barry Alvarez as head coach in 1990, the most glorious era in Wisconsin football was widely regarded to be the seven years under Ivan B. Williamson from 1949 to 1955.

The Badgers won one Big Ten Conference title during that stretch and went to their first Rose Bowl in 1953. But they were in contention for a title in all but Williamson's final season, and his 41–19–4 record was the second-best in the conference over that stretch.

Besides the 1952 title, the Badgers were within one victory of the conference championship in 1949, 1950, 1951, 1953 and 1954. But it was usually the same thing standing in their way—Ohio State.

The major nemesis for Williamson was the Buckeyes, who had the conference's best record over that span at 46–15–4. Williamson was 0–6–1 against Ohio State, and losses in 1950, 1952 and 1953 deprived Wisconsin of undisputed conference championships. The Badgers could have tied for the title in 1949 and 1954 if not for losses to the Buckeyes.

Williamson was an impressive 29–13–4 in Big Ten games, including 29–7–3 against conference teams other than Ohio State. It was the best stretch at Wisconsin since John. R. Richards went 29–9–4 in 1911, 1917 and 1919–1922.

Sportswriters in the state were surprised by the choice of the man known as Ivy, or "Red," who was two weeks shy of his 38th birthday when he was hired on January 24, 1949.

Harry A. Stuhldreher resigned on December 11, 1948, following a 2–7 season, after growing tired of signs reading "Goodbye Harry" in the student section. Bud Wilkinson, the coach at Oklahoma, had refused overtures from Wisconsin, with a touch of disdain that insulted Badger fans, reportedly citing the "conditions" at the university.

George Svendsen, the Minnesota line coach, was regarded as "a cinch for the post." Lisle Blackbourn, the Wisconsin backfield coach, was regarded as the second choice.

But Williamson's credentials were impeccable. He was born in Prairie Depot (later changed to Wayne), Ohio, and attended high school in Bowling Green. He played football and basketball at Michigan, despite an earlier ankle injury that reportedly caused a doctor to tell him, "It would be foolhardy for you ever to play football again."

He was a football star at Michigan from 1930 to 1932, when the Wolverines lost one game, and was an All–Big Ten end and captain as a senior. He won the Gold Medal, presented to the outstanding gentleman, athlete and scholar, in the Class of 1933, and graduated with high distinction.

His coach at Michigan, Harry Kipke, said, "Ivan Williamson is the smartest player I have ever had or hope to have."

One of his college teammates was future president Gerald Ford, and the two were also assistant coaches together at Yale. Williamson was an assistant at Yale from 1934 to 1941, returning in 1945 after a hitch in the navy.

He was the head coach at Lafayette College in Easton, Pennsylvania, for two years, with records of 6–3 and 7–2, before coming to Wisconsin. His second year, the only losses were to Army and Rutgers.

"I will give Wisconsin the best football possible" was all Williamson would promise to the *Milwaukee Journal Sentinel*.

His offense was modeled after the Yale-T, with some variations. He was praised for innovation and willingness to adapt to the players at hand. He was in favor of the controversial two-platoon system.

In his first year he took a team not highly regarded in the preseason and had it in Rose Bowl contention going into the final game. That started a couple of trends. In Williamson's first three seasons, the Badgers steadily improved each year and had a chance to win the title going into the last game, only to fall short.

"Each year he told fans not to expect a championship," read a United Press International story. "Each year they got a whiff of roses—just enough to keep them keyed up."

Williamson's teams had success on both sides of the football. The 1951 team might have had the best defense in school history, the famed "Hard Rocks" who were the nation's top-ranked overall defense. The offense was wide open and featured outstanding passers in John Coatta, the future coach, and Jim Haluska.

The Badgers missed the 1951 title only because of a heartbreaking 14–10 loss to Illinois and finished 7–1–1. The following year Williamson took the Badgers to their only No. 1 ranking in school history after beating Illinois 20–6 in the second game, only to lose to Ohio State, as usual, 23–14 the following week.

Even though a 21–21 tie with Minnesota in the final game prevented an undisputed title, the Badgers' 5–2–1 Big Ten record was enough for their first trip to Pasadena, California.

The winning combination that year was Haluska, the sophomore quarterback who started the season at the bottom of the depth chart; halfback Harland Carl, "flashing speed and deception"; and a sophomore fullback named Alan "the Horse" Ameche, who "charges the line like a wild stallion."

The coach was in line for some praise, too, heading to the Rose Bowl. "Tremendously popular with his players and is idolized by his staff associates," it was written in one Associated Press story. "The harmonious picture is a major factor in the Badgers' success."

The Badgers dominated the Rose Bowl from a statistical standpoint but lost 7–0 to Southern California. Led by Ameche's 133 rushing yards, the Badgers outgained USC by 120 total yards, including a 211–48 advantage on the ground. But Wisconsin just couldn't score.

"We played up to our ability," Williamson said afterward. "We just didn't have enough to make the scores. They were too good for us today."

Williamson had used the formula devised by Stuhldreher in 1942 to build a Big Ten contender, recruiting the best from Wisconsin and northern Illinois, including Chicago. Of the 43 primary players on the 1952 title team, 26 were from Wisconsin, 12 were from Illinois, two each from Michigan and Ohio and one from Kentucky.

Williamson's only losing season came in 1955 when the Badgers were 4–5 overall.

There was no pressure on the popular football coach to step down, but after athletic director Guy Sundt passed away unexpectedly on October 25, 1955, Williamson was reportedly "happy" to take over that job and leave the coaching to Milt Bruhn, his top assistant and line coach, who came with him from Lafayette in 1949.

Williamson's tenure as athletic director had plenty of good and bad. The Athletic Department grew to unprecedented heights under him, just as the Badgers football fortunes had soared under his direction.

During his 13 years as athletic director, Wisconsin built the Natatorium and Camp Randall Memorial Building, expanded Camp Randall Stadium seating capacity twice to 77,280, renovated the press box and installed "Tartan Turf" on the field.

Williamson was regarded as a champion of "minor" sports. At a time when there were financial reasons for dropping some non-income-producing sports, he revived the men's hockey program, which grew to become one of the best in the nation and gave Wisconsin a strong third revenue sport, along with football and men's basketball.

He was also a strong voice in the conference and served as chairman of the national football rules committee for five years at a time when rules were adopted to make the college game safer and more exciting.

Most of his problems coincided with the decline of the football program under Bruhn, starting in 1964. That was a time of rising costs, and a steady decline in football attendance that decade led to financial problems.

It was also a time of growing social unrest on the Madison campus. Late in Williamson's tenure as athletic director, 18 black athletes boycotted the annual football banquet and presented the Athletic Department with a list of grievances.

The final straw probably came when a projected $778,000 profit for football in 1968 was actually a $261,053 deficit. Williamson was fired on January 10, 1969, and reassigned as professor of athletics.

He never got to serve in his new role because he died one month and three days later, at age 58, after falling down the basement steps of his home in Madison. He was carrying a glass casserole full of soup to the downstairs freezer when he fell. He suffered irreversible brain stem damage due to the head injury, according to a hospital spokesman.

It was the same day Elroy Hirsch, his eventual successor as athletic director, arrived in town to be interviewed by the committee screening candidates.

Even though the football fortunes waned during the end of his time as athletic director, Williamson was the coach, more than any other, who was given credit for revitalizing the program during the glorious 1950s and early 1960s, when the team went to three Rose Bowls. He got the entire state of Wisconsin excited about football again.

"Under his hands as coach, the Wisconsin football team rose to one of its proudest periods," UW chancellor Edwin Young said following Williamson's death. "As athletic director he expanded the university's intercollegiate competition and strengthened the sports programs for all. He was an athlete, a teacher and an athletic leader, and Wisconsin will long remember and sorely miss his contributions."

DAVE McCLAIN
1978–1985
46–42–3, three bowl games (1981
Garden State, 1982 Independence,
1984 Hall of Fame)

It's one of the great unanswered questions for the Wisconsin football program. Could Dave McClain have been the coach to get the Badgers back to the Rose Bowl, had he not died of a heart attack at age 48 on April 28, 1986?

McClain brought winning football and bowl games back to Wisconsin after nearly a two-decade absence but sadly never got the chance to answer that question.

This much is known: McClain, who spent eight years as head coach, had the Badgers on the right path. Wisconsin's appearance in the 1981 Garden State Bowl against Tennessee was the first for the program since the 1963 Rose Bowl and started a stretch of three bowls in four years under McClain.

Starting in 1981, Wisconsin had four straight seven-win seasons. The last coach to post four straight winning seasons was Ivy Williamson from 1951 to 1954.

The talent level in the program rose dramatically under McClain. High school coaches in the state never warmed to his predecessor, John Jardine, but they quickly embraced McClain. Jardine's teams featured wide-open offenses but little in the way of defense. McClain built strong defenses around many in-state products, like nose guard Tim Krumrie, safeties Matt VandenBoom and David Greenwood and linebackers Rick Graf and Tim Jordan.

The Badgers had six players selected in the 1983 draft and a record 11 players, including three first-rounders, in the 12-round 1985 draft, following McClain's last season.

McClain learned as an assistant coach under two Big Ten icons, coaching under Bo Schembechler at Miami (Ohio) from 1963 to 1966, before Schembechler went on to fame at Michigan, and under Woody Hayes at Ohio State from 1969 to 1970.

Perhaps it was that experience that helped the Badgers end long dry spells against the Big Ten's two most prominent programs. In 1981 Wisconsin defeated top-ranked Michigan in the season opener for the first time since 1962. It also knocked off Ohio State for the first time since 1959 and only the second time since 1944. Along with a victory over Purdue that season, it marked the first time in school history Wisconsin defeated those three opponents in the same year.

McClain's teams defeated Ohio State four of his last five years, including two rare victories on the road in Columbus, Ohio.

But McClain never got the chance to finish what he started. He was in a sauna, following a workout, two days after the conclusion of spring practice, when he suffered the heart attack he long had feared might be coming. His father, mother and older brother also died of heart attacks.

Greg Thomas was a safety who was a part of McClain's final recruiting class but never got a chance to play for him. Instead Thomas played for three different coaches—Jim Hilles, who was McClain's defensive coordinator and served as the interim coach in 1986, followed by Don Morton and then Barry Alvarez. That class quickly saw its hopes vanish of contending for Big Ten titles and building on McClain's success.

"You think, 'We've got a chance to do something pretty special here,'" Thomas said many years later of his feeling after signing with the Badgers. "Then Coach McClain passed away, and the program was sent into disarray."

In the aftermath of McClain's tragic death, some fans tended to gloss over the shortcomings of his tenure. From 1977 through 1985, McClain's teams had a losing record in Big Ten games (32–34–3), landed on probation twice (1982 and 1983), went 1–2 in bowl games and were beaten by 25 points or more 11 times.

Despite the talent in the program, it looked like Wisconsin had reached a seven-win ceiling, although McClain thought the 1986 team had a chance to be his best, with 10 senior starters on defense.

The previous season, when the Badgers went 5–6, had been a bitter disappointment for McClain. His solution? Work even harder. Already known for putting in long days,

McClain pushed himself even harder. "If you're not going to put your heart and soul into coaching, you're not going to make it," McClain said. "I really believe that."

McClain poured his heart into coaching. Born in Upper Sandusky, Ohio, he was a down-to-earth, unassuming Midwesterner. He loved everything about coaching, including recruiting, which some head coaches despise. He especially liked sitting in living rooms and kitchens, talking to recruits. "That might have been his forte," the *Wisconsin State Journal*'s Tom Butler wrote after McClain's death. "Dave McClain was down home."

The Big Ten Coach of the Year award was named after McClain following his death, along with Wisconsin's indoor practice facility, which opened in 1988 and also includes locker rooms, training facilities, the Fetzer Learning Center and a spacious weight room.

Needless to say, the players were crushed by McClain's death. "Why someone so good?" senior linebacker Craig Raddatz said. "He cared."

Hilles had the unenviable task of trying to pick up the pieces. That was followed by the hiring of Morton, which sent the program in a further downward spiral until Barry Alvarez arrived in 1990. Three years later—and seven years after McClain's death—the Badgers were finally back in the Rose Bowl.

"We lost more than an outstanding coach," athletic director Elroy Hirsch said at the time of McClain's death. "He was a great father, husband and human being. People like this are not replaced."

MILT BRUHN
1956–1966
52–45–6
Big Ten titles in 1959 and 1962
Rose Bowls in 1960 and 1963

If Badger fans didn't fully appreciate it at the time Milt Bruhn was coaching, all they had to do was wait a few years to comprehend the accomplishments of the football team during that time.

Bruhn was head coach at Wisconsin for 11 years and had a record of 52–45–6. He was the first coach to take the Badgers to two Rose Bowls, and in a wonderful span from 1957 to 1959, his teams went 20–7–1, the best years at the school since the turn of the century. Three of his teams finished the season ranked in the top 10.

Yet, because it didn't end well for Bruhn, who went 8–19–2 in his final three years (1964 to 1966), his legacy was tarnished a bit in the eyes of some fans. But in the three decades of struggles that followed the Badgers' appearance in the 1963 Rose Bowl, it became clear that the first half of Bruhn's tenure was a special time, indeed.

"I think his stature has grown the longer he's been gone," Pat Richter, who played for Bruhn from 1960 to 1962, said following his coach's death in 1991. "I think his players appreciated him as a man and as a coach, but I'm not sure if the public fully appreciated his coaching."

The Badgers defeated Minnesota 11–7 in the final regular-season game in 1959 to win their first undisputed Big Ten title since 1912. That team was led by All–Big Ten quarterback Dale Hackbart and All–Big Ten guard Jerry Stalcup. Despite a 44–8 loss to Washington in the Rose Bowl, Wisconsin finished No. 6 in both major polls.

The 1962 team, led by quarterback Ron Vander Kelen and Richter, a consensus All-American end, went 8–1 in the regular season and lost, 42–37, to Southern California in the 1963 Rose Bowl, which is still considered one of college football's classic games. That team finished the season ranked No. 2, the highest in school history.

Bruhn was a burly man who was the starting left guard at Minnesota for Bernie Bierman on the 1934 national championship team. But his players regarded him as a gentleman, a down-to-earth coach who treated his players like family.

Ivy Williamson brought Bruhn with him to Wisconsin from Lafayette College in Easton, Pennsylvania, in 1949 as his top assistant. When Williamson stepped up to be the athletic director following the 1955 season, Bruhn, recognized as one of the outstanding line coaches in the Big Ten, was the obvious replacement.

Bruhn's teams played the split-T offense, installed with the assistance of then–Oklahoma Coach Bud Wilkinson, a former Golden Gophers player and a friend of Bruhn's.

The 1961 Badgers led the nation in passing, averaging 188.4 yards per game, and the 1962 team averaged 31.7 points a game to lead the nation.

Some of his peers were Bump Elliott, Murray Warmath and Woody Hayes—coaches who evoke the essence of hard-hitting Big Ten–style football—and Bruhn beat them regularly.

The trouble for Bruhn started in 1964, when the remaining former Williamson assistants on his staff were kicked upstairs to Athletic Department administrative posts. But the addition of young blood on the staff could not save Bruhn.

It was a time of growing financial problems in the Athletic Department and a deepening disconnect between the university and the athletic programs. Bruhn ultimately resigned in 1966, under pressure, after three straight losing seasons. "From the day you're hired, you know it's going to happen to you some day," Bruhn recalled in 1989.

He stayed at UW for 12 more years, the last five as director of the Nielsen Tennis Stadium, before retiring in 1978. He once told his wife, Helen, before coming to Madison, that he would like to stay a dozen or so years. He worked at UW for 30 years.

He was a private man who kept a low profile—possibly too low, because it allowed people to forget what he accomplished. But Bruhn was one of 35 charter members inducted into the UW Athletic Hall of Fame. He was in a wheelchair when he received the award, not too long before his death, and reports said it was Bruhn who got the biggest applause of the evening when his accomplishments were read. He finally received the appreciation he deserved.

Milt Bruhn (left) jokes with USC football coach John McKay less than two weeks after USC beat Wisconsin, 42–37, in the 1963 Rose Bowl.

"I will always remember what a gentleman he was," said Jim Bakken, a kicker for Bruhn from 1959 to 1961, who went on to a long NFL career and later served as a UW associate athletic director. "I think his personality was reflected in his coaching."

1896 Badgers

1897 Badgers

1901 Badgers

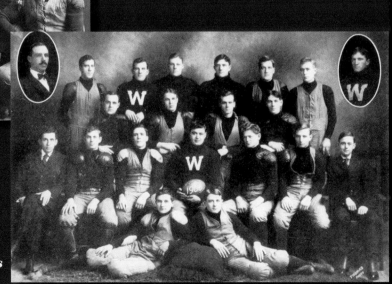

1906 Badgers

Badger Superlatives

Wisconsin football history is littered with moments of greatness—championships won, great games played, superior individual efforts, memorable upsets and more. Here is a small sample of that record of achievement.

THE GREAT TEAMS

1896, 1897, 1901

Wisconsin captured the first two titles in the Western Conference, led by coach Phil King and a tough defense that registered shutouts in six of seven victories while going 7–1–1 to win the inaugural title in 1896. The only loss was 18–8, to the Carlisle Indians, in the final game, which was played indoors at the Chicago Coliseum and was the first night game in school history. The following season, Wisconsin registered eight shutouts on its way to a 9–1 record. The only loss was 6–0 against the UW Alumni. Australian kicker Pat O'Dea, the famed "Kangaroo Kicker," kicked 14 field goals, and the Badgers won their second title under King, who had a 65–11–1 record in eight seasons (1896–1902, 1905) and has the best career winning percentage (.851) in school history going into the 2006 season. King won his third and final Western Conference championship in 1901 as the Badgers went 9–0 and outscored their opposition 317–5. However, the season did include two wins over high school teams.

1906

Traditional league powers Minnesota, Michigan and Chicago were missing from the Wisconsin schedule due to a faculty reform movement. But the Badgers, under Dr. C.P. Hutchins, posted Western Conference wins over Iowa, Illinois and Purdue by a combined 63–15 and tied for the conference title with the Gophers.

1912

The Badgers posted their third undefeated season, concluding with a 28–10 win at Iowa under coach William Juneau. It was the last undefeated season in Wisconsin history. Led by consensus All-America tackle Robert "Butts" Butler, the Badgers set a school record with nine players on the All–Western Conference team, registered four shutouts and allowed only 29 points.

1912 Badgers

1942

Wisconsin didn't win the conference title under Harry Stuhldreher, finishing 8–1–1, but this still is regarded as one of the best teams in school history. It featured halfback Elroy "Crazylegs" Hirsch, All-America end Dave Schreiner and fullback Pat Harder. The season was played against the backdrop of World War II, with many of the Badgers knowing they would be heading off to the military when the school year was over. Wisconsin tied Notre Dame 7–7 in the second game, then knocked off top-ranked Ohio State 17–7 on homecoming. But the following week the Badgers suffered their only loss, 6–0, at Iowa. The first half ended in controversy, with Harder believing he had scored a touchdown on a dive play. The linesman signaled a touchdown but was overruled by the referee. Following that disappointment, the offense couldn't get untracked in the second half. Hirsch was held to 37 yards on 21 carries.

1951

A local sportswriter named the defense "the Hard Rocks," and the unit lived up to the tough moniker, leading the country in yards allowed (154.8 per game) and finishing second in rushing defense (66.8 yards per game). The defense only allowed 5.9 points per game and outscored opponents 58–53. The defense was such a hit that the Athletic Department received a letter from a fan requesting that the Badgers punt on first down so he could see more of the defense. Eight of the nine seniors on defense scored in their careers. But a 14–10 loss at Illinois in the Big Ten opener, in which Wisconsin had more first downs (20–8), more plays (77–46) and more total yardage (274–142), cost the Badgers the title as they finished 7–1–1.

1952

The Badgers had been close to winning conference titles in the first three years under Ivy Williamson, and they finally broke through in his fourth year. After beating Illinois 20–6 in the conference opener, they were ranked No. 1 in the nation for the first time in school history, only to lose 23–14 to Ohio State the following week. The defense was not nearly as strong as the previous year, and a 21–21 tie with Minnesota in the final regular-season game cost Wisconsin the undisputed title. Paul Giel, Minnesota's triple-threat tailback, dazzled the Badgers, running for 85 yards and passing for 167. Neither the Wisconsin players nor the fans showed much emotion filing out of Camp Randall Stadium that afternoon, after finishing tied with Purdue atop the conference at 4–1–1. The two teams did not meet that season, so Wisconsin got the Rose Bowl bid in a 7–3 vote of conference athletic directors the following day, on the strength of its 6–2–1 overall record, compared with Purdue's 4–3–2. That sent the Badgers to their first Rose Bowl, where they lost, 7–0, to Southern California.

1959

The season did not start out well for Wisconsin. The Badgers lost 21–0 on a muddy field at Purdue, which had gone 0–9–1 in its previous 10 games against Wisconsin. But the following week, Wisconsin bounced back with a 25–16 victory over Iowa, the defending Big Ten champion, followed by wins over perennial powers Ohio State and Michigan. The Badgers were led by quarterback Dale Hackbart, who would go on to play 14 seasons in the NFL as a defensive back, and a strong and fast line that included Jerry Stalcup, a guard who was named the team's Most Valuable Player, and unanimous All-America tackle Dan Lanphear. The Rose Bowl turned out to be a disaster; Wisconsin lost to Washington 44–8.

1952 Badgers

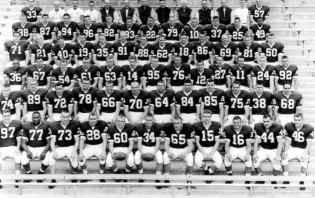

1959 Badgers

1962

With Ron Vander Kelen throwing and Pat Richter catching, Wisconsin knocked off top-ranked Northwestern 37–6 and made it to the Rose Bowl for the second time in four years under coach Milt Bruhn. A 14–9 victory over Minnesota to finish the regular season 8–1 clinched their second-place rank in the polls. The clutch play of Vander Kelen was a big reason Wisconsin scored every time it was inside its opponents' 20-yard line leading up to the Rose Bowl. Then, in the Rose Bowl came one of the greatest college football games ever played. Southern California led 42–14 after the first play of the fourth quarter, but Vander Kelen and the Badgers refused to surrender. Vander Kelen, who set a Rose Bowl record with 401 passing yards, led the Badgers to 23 straight points before they ran out of time in the Trojans' 42–37 victory.

1962 Badgers

1981

Wisconsin had managed only two winning seasons in the previous 17 years. But things were about to change in the fourth season under coach Dave McClain. That was evident in the opening game when the Badgers, who were outscored 176–0 in their four previous games against Michigan, shocked the top-ranked Wolverines 21–14 at Camp Randall Stadium. McClain, an assistant on Michigan coach Bo Schembechler's staff at Miami (Ohio) in the early 1960s, and his players had grown weary of the beatings. Wisconsin dominated the game, with a 439–229 edge in total yardage. The Badgers appeared to have destiny on their side when they defeated Purdue 35–31 three weeks later, scoring two touchdowns in the final 1:29, including the game-winner when linebacker Jim Melka picked up a blocked punt and returned it 30 yards. The next week, another giant fell when Wisconsin defeated No. 18 Ohio State 24–21.

Unfortunately, the Badgers wasted the 3–0 start in the Big Ten with back-to-back losses to Michigan State and Illinois but still finished 7–5 overall, the first of four straight winning seasons. They ended an 18-year streak without a bowl with a trip to the Garden State Bowl, where they lost to Tennessee 28–21.

1982

Going into Columbus, Ohio, on October 9, a place where the Badgers had not won since 1918, and shutting out the Buckeyes 6–0 with a defense that ranked last in the Big Ten has to rank with the biggest upsets in Wisconsin history. A steady rain fell during the game, and UW junior quarterback Randy Wright suffered a thumb injury in the first quarter, but the Badgers scored the game's only touchdown and chewed up the final 8:33 of the contest with a 17-play drive, all on the ground. Wisconsin capped the season with a 14–3 victory over Kansas State in the Independence Bowl, the first bowl victory in school history. Wright threw two touchdowns, and the defense limited Kansas State to 192 total yards in a game played in Shreveport, Louisiana, with 23 mph winds and below-zero temperatures.

1993

Tragedy and triumph, real-life heroes and a coveted Rose Bowl appearance clinched halfway around the world in Tokyo, Japan—this season had it all. It started with a stunning 13–10 victory over Michigan that turned tragic when an estimated 12,000 fans in the student section at Camp Randall Stadium attempted to storm the field at the same time. More than 70 people were injured when the surge, described as "a human tidal wave," crushed them against a bottom railing and a chain-link fence.

Miraculously, nobody died, thanks in no small part to the efforts of several players, who waded into the crowd to help the tangled mass of students. Among the heroes was Michael Brin, a walk-on wide receiver on the scout team who later became an emergency-room doctor. He rescued one female student, who was close to passing out at the bottom of the pile, and briefly administered mouth-to-mouth resuscitation to another student.

The following week, the Badgers tied No. 3 Ohio State 14–14 when Rick Schnetzky's 33-yard game-winning field goal attempt was blocked. But the Badgers' Rose Bowl hopes were put back in their own hands after Michigan crushed the Buckeyes 28–0.

The final regular-season game against Michigan State was supposed to be a home game, but UW officials had agreed the previous

1993 Badgers

year to move it to the Tokyo Dome. The trip was worthwhile, Wisconsin won 41–20 and an enthusiastic crowd of 10,000 greeted the weary travelers when they returned home.

Coach Barry Alvarez had taken the Badgers to heights—not to mention places—they'd never been before, and they capped it off with the first Rose Bowl victory in school history, 21–16 over favored UCLA. Wisconsin set a school record for wins, going 10–1–1, and the Big Ten title it shared with Ohio State was its first since 1962. UW had eight first-team all-conference players, including Brent Moss, the Big Ten and Rose Bowl Most Valuable Player.

1998

Wisconsin didn't win any style points in 1998 with an offense that regarded the passing game as a nuisance. This was old-school football—line them up and knock them down, and throw in a heavy dose of defense. But it worked.

Wisconsin opened the season with nine straight wins then got mauled 27–10 at Michigan. But just like they did in the previous

Rose Bowl season, when the Badgers got a late-season break, they took full advantage of some help from the Buckeyes. This time, Ohio State knocked off Michigan 31–16, and Wisconsin's defense, which ranked first in the nation in scoring defense, dominated Penn State in a 24–3 victory.

This was an opportunistic team, leading the nation in turnover margin, too. Defensive end Tom Burke led the nation in sacks, and cornerback Jamar Fletcher was tops in interceptions. It was the winningest season in school history, both in terms of wins and winning percentage, at 11–1. Tailback Ron Dayne rushed for 246 yards in the Rose Bowl as UW enjoyed another matchup with UCLA, winning this one 38–31.

1999

This might have been Barry Alvarez's best overall team—the Badgers led the Big Ten in scoring offense and defense—although it didn't look that way early in the season. It took the Badgers four games to find a quarterback, but

1998 Badgers

redshirt freshman Brooks Bollinger emerged in the fourth quarter of a loss to Michigan that dropped UW to 2–2 overall. Bollinger was named the starter, and UW won its next eight Big Ten games by an average of 22.3 points. The only close calls were a 20–17 overtime victory at Minnesota, which Alvarez watched from a hospital bed after undergoing knee-replacement surgery that couldn't wait until the end of the season, and a 28–21 win at Purdue, where tailback Ron Dayne emerged as the Heisman Trophy favorite over Boilermakers quarterback Drew Brees by rushing for 222 yards in the Badgers' victory. Wisconsin became the first Big Ten team in history to win back-to-back Rose Bowls, defeating Stanford 17–9. Dayne won the Heisman, broke the Division I-A career rushing record and was the consensus National Player of the Year.

2005

When Barry Alvarez announced in July that the upcoming season would be his last as football coach, there were questions about what kind of send-off he would get. Wisconsin returned only 10 of the players who had started the bowl game the previous season and had several huge holes to fill. But with the help of tailback Brian Calhoun, a transfer from Colorado who sat out the previous season, the players made sure Alvarez got the send-off he deserved.

The defense allowed 417.4 yards per game, the most in school history. But the offense set a school record by averaging 34.3 points per game, and Calhoun became only the second Division I-A player to finish with at least 1,500 rushing yards (1,636) and 500 receiving yards (571) in the same season.

After consecutive bowl losses to Southeastern Conference opponents, Alvarez went out on a high note with a convincing 24–10 victory over Auburn in the Capital One Bowl to finish his career with an 8–3 bowl record.

2006

Bret Bielema, 36, the second-youngest coach in Division I-A, could not have set the bar much higher in his first year as head coach. The Badgers, picked to finish in the middle of the Big Ten, went 12–1, setting a school record for victories, and won the Capital One Bowl for a second straight year with a 17–14 victory over favored Arkansas.

Bielema had three essential building blocks: a fifth-year senior quarterback in John Stocco, an outstanding defense that ranked third nationally in the regular season and a favorable schedule, which included an easy slate of non-conference opponents and did not include conference champion Ohio State.

While Bielema's first year certainly raised expectations around the program, former UW coach Barry Alvarez said it beat the way he started. "I'd rather start out 11–1 (regular season) than 1–10," Alvarez, the current UW athletic director, said of his first season at the school in 1990. "He'll recruit better. People know his plan works. For a young guy to be that successful, he's got a good nucleus coming back, he's got his program set. He did a (heck) of a job putting a new staff together, walking in and having the year he did."

THE BOWLS: GREAT PERFORMANCES

1963 ROSE BOWL
January 1, 1963, Pasadena, California
Southern California 42, Wisconsin 37

For the longest time, this loss stood as probably the greatest—and surely most famous—football game in Wisconsin history. But this was no ordinary loss. How many times in a big game does the losing team get all the recognition and credit? And deserve every bit of it?

That's what happened when No. 2 Wisconsin met No. 1 Southern California in what remains one of the most memorable Rose Bowl games ever played. The Trojans escaped with the victory, but it was the Badgers' incredible rally that captured the attention of college football fans across the country.

The game had a touch of controversy, too, especially for Wisconsin fans. The start was delayed 15 minutes while UW players stood around on the field with a couple of marching bands. USC, which apparently was provided a different pregame schedule, came out of the locker room later.

The Badgers and coach Milt Bruhn were already feeling the heat, which had nothing to do with the California weather. There was grumbling that the team had lacked focus and treated the trip to Pasadena, California, three years earlier like a vacation, the result being a 44–8 loss to Washington. Bruhn responded by sequestering the team in spartan surroundings,

at the Order of Passionate Fathers Monastery in the Sierra Madre Mountains, far from the glitz and glamour of Los Angeles.

Nevertheless, the Badgers got off to a lousy start, with the help of a couple controversial calls. The Trojans' Bill Nelson appeared to lose a fumble in the second quarter, with Wisconsin recovering, but the play was ruled dead. Bruhn could only fume as the Trojans scored two plays later to take a 21–7 second-quarter lead.

Just before halftime Wisconsin quarterback Ron Vander Kelen hit halfback Louis Holland for what appeared to be a 30-yard touchdown, but the play was called back because of a clip.

After the first play of the third quarter, USC's lead had grown to a seemingly insurmountable 42–14. But Wisconsin and Vander Kelen were just getting started. At a time when potent passing games were still a novelty in the college game, Vander Kelen set UW and Rose Bowl records with 401 passing yards, on the way to being named the game's MVP. Pat Richter caught 11 passes for 163 yards. The teams' 79 total points set a Rose Bowl record that lasted for 28 years.

Wisconsin scored the last 23 points and had the ball 60 yards away from a winning touchdown, but after fielding a punt, Holland was tackled as time ran out. Two days later, the headline on the *Chicago Tribune*'s wrap-up story said it all: "Badgers needed just one more play."

Ron Vander Kelen's epic 401-yard passing performance in the 1963 Rose Bowl will live forever in college football lore.

1982 INDEPENDENCE BOWL
December 11, 1982, Shreveport, Louisiana
Wisconsin 14, Kansas State 3

It was hardly a thing of beauty, but the Badgers finally won a bowl game for the first time in school history. A crowd of only 24,684 fans showed up in terrible conditions, with 23 mph winds and temperatures that dropped to 10 degrees below zero.

The game featured five turnovers, 14 punts, 22 completions in 59 attempts (.372) and 14 penalties. Randy Wright threw two touchdown passes for Wisconsin, and his 87-yard completion to Tim Stracka set a record for the bowl game.

Badgers nose guard Tim Krumrie was the defensive most valuable player, helping hold Kansas State to 65 rushing yards on 33 carries.

"Wisconsin wasn't supposed to win the Rose Bowl. People laughed at me when I put up the sign, 'The Road to the Rose Bowl starts here.'"

—BARRY ALVAREZ, WHO EARNED
SWEET VINDICATION WITH THE BADGERS'
ROSE BOWL WIN OVER UCLA

1994 ROSE BOWL
January 1, 1994, Pasadena, California
Wisconsin 21, UCLA 16

It was a moment that took your breath away. Anybody who had endured even part of the misery that had been the Wisconsin football program for the previous 30 years had to be moved, standing on the field prior to the Rose Bowl and seeing more than 70,000 fans in that famous stadium clad in Badgers red.

Al Fish, Athletic Department administrative officer at the time, described the moment: "At that very minute, the (UW)

A new era in Badger football history dawns, as Brent Moss runs wild in the Badgers' 21–16 Rose Bowl win over UCLA.

On January 1, 1994, the Rose Bowl became "Camp Randall West," and the Badgers didn't disappoint their legion of fans who made the trek to Los Angeles.

band came out at the beginning of the Rose Bowl, as they traditionally do, coming through the goal posts. That's when it hit, for me, because up until then it was just kind of a whirlwind of chaos and late nights and phone calls.

"We all tried to act like we had been there before. For the most part, I think we succeeded. But most of us, obviously, had never been there before. It was thrilling in a special way, which probably could never be repeated, unless we go another 30 years sometime without going to a big bowl."

Fortunately for the Badgers, head coach Barry Alvarez was one of the few, along with athletic director Pat Richter, to have been there before. Alvarez refused to let the upstart Badgers be pushed around or intimidated.

It started before the Badgers even qualified for the game. Fish attended a planning meeting in California when other school officials were in Tokyo preparing for the game against Michigan State, which Wisconsin needed to win to go to the Rose Bowl for the first time in 31 years.

Fish had received orders from Alvarez, who was in his fourth year at UW. Alvarez knew the lay of the land, having gone to the Rose Bowl twice as an assistant coach at Iowa. In the room were more than 60 people, including Rose Bowl officials, a large group of representatives from UCLA, which had secured its berth in the game, and Fish.

It was the Big Ten Conference's turn to be in the home locker room. But since UCLA plays its home games in the Rose Bowl, it had requested to stay in its locker room. Fish was instructed by Alvarez not to give up the home locker room.

"So, in this room full of UCLA people and Rose Bowl people and one Wisconsin guy, who had never been to a bowl game, they asked that question," said Fish. "I stood up and said, 'No, if we win (in Tokyo), we will want the home locker room, and besides that, we want all UCLA markings painted over, or covered, before we go in the locker room.'

"And there was this giant hush over the room. UCLA people were really upset that these brash Badgers would send some rookie who had no idea what he was doing, then had the temerity to kick them out of their own locker room, before they even knew they were playing in the game."

The Badgers followed Alvarez's lead and made themselves at home in "Camp Randall West."

Tailback Brent Moss, the game's MVP, rushed for 158 yards on 36 carries and scored two first-half touchdowns as the Badgers built a 14–3 lead. It was 21–10 after quarterback Darrell Bevell recorded the game's signature play. Not finding a receiver open, Bevell took off on what appeared to be a slow-motion 21-yard run for the game-clinching touchdown.

Ten years later, Alvarez was able to put that game in the proper perspective. "Wisconsin wasn't supposed to win the Rose Bowl," he said. "People laughed at me when I put up the sign, 'The Road to the Rose Bowl starts here.'

"I think more than anything else, that game gave our program credibility. Not only the fact that you could win the league, but you could go to the West Coast and play the Pac-10's best team and beat them."

1995 HALL OF FAME BOWL
January 2, 1995, Tampa, Florida
Wisconsin 34, Duke 20

Senior Terrell Fletcher rushed for 241 yards, and the Badgers intercepted three passes in the first half, with Jeff Messenger scoring on a 19-yard return, as the Badgers won their second January bowl game in as many years. More than 30,000 UW fans made the trip and watched as the Blue Devils pulled within 27–20, then saw Fletcher break loose on third-and-1 for a 49-yard touchdown romp to seal the win.

1996 COPPER BOWL
December 27, 1996, Tucson, Arizona
Wisconsin 38, Utah 10

The Ron Dayne train was rolling, and there was no way Utah was going to stop it. Dayne concluded a remarkable freshman season with 246 yards and three touchdowns, as the Badgers throttled the Utes. The expected matchup between Dayne and Utah's Chris Fuamatu-Ma'afala, the nation's two largest running backs, never got off the ground as the Utah runner hurt his ankle in the first quarter.

In Dayne's final three games of the season, against Illinois, Hawaii and Utah, he rushed 107 times for 874 yards (8.2 average), with 11 touchdowns. Counting the bowl game, he finished with 2,109 yards, the eighth-best total in NCAA history (although the NCAA did not count bowl games at the time). His 1,863 regular-season yards broke Herschel Walker's freshman record, set at Georgia in 1980, of 1,616 yards.

1999 ROSE BOWL
January 1, 1999, Pasadena, California
Wisconsin 38, UCLA 31

The Badgers got all the motivation they needed, thanks to a nationally televised insult from CBS analyst Craig James, who called them, "the worst team I can remember playing in the Rose Bowl."

Wisconsin coach Barry Alvarez smiled the first time he heard about James's comment. Nobody was better at playing the "no respect"

Dayne silenced any doubters with a 246-yard, four-touchdown showcase in the 1999 Rose Bowl.

card than Alvarez, whose team had defeated UCLA in the Rose Bowl as seven-point under-dogs five years earlier.

That season the Badgers had been per-ceived as a feel-good story, given their 31-year wait between Rose Bowls. This time, they seemed to be punching bags for the national media, which relished in poking fun at their supposed blandness.

UCLA was expecting to play for the national championship in the Fiesta Bowl, before losing 49–45 to Miami, which snapped a 20-game winning streak. The Bruins allowed a whopping 689 total yards in that game, and that porous defense was again their undoing against Wisconsin.

Badger tailback Ron Dayne rumbled for 246 yards and four touchdowns, and redshirt freshman cornerback Jamar Fletcher had a pivotal 46-yard interception return for a touch-down in the fourth quarter. Wisconsin's defense also got a stop on UCLA's final posses-sion, with freshman defensive tackle Wendell Bryant sacking Cade McNown on fourth down.

After making believers out of everybody, Alvarez had the last word in response to James's comment, saying "Well, I know we're at least the second-worst."

"The worst team I can remember playing in the Rose Bowl."

— ANALYST CRAIG JAMES ON WISCONSIN, PRIOR TO THE 1999 ROSE BOWL

"Well, I know we're at least the second-worst."

— BARRY ALVAREZ, AFTER THE BADGERS BEAT UCLA 38–31

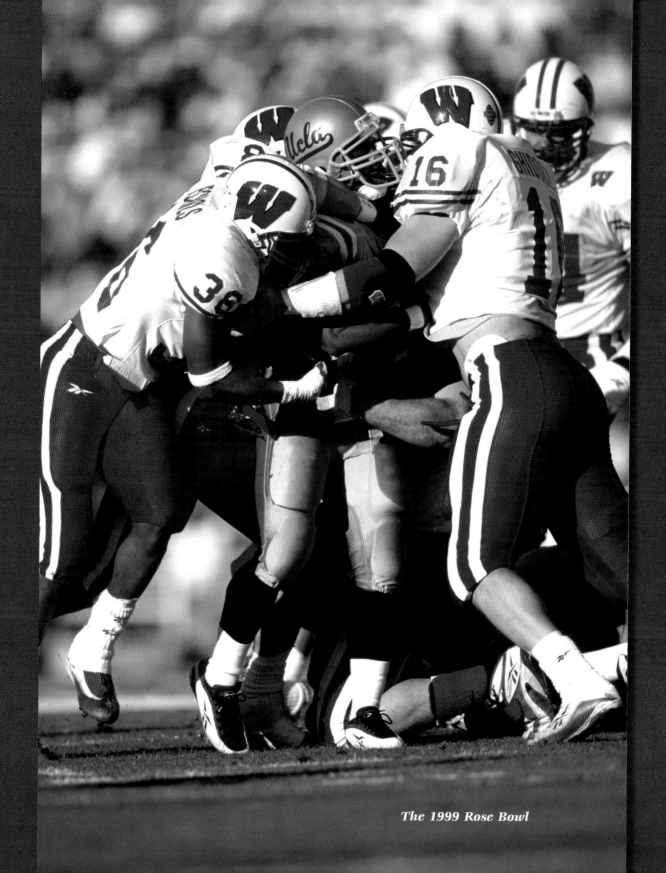

The 1999 Rose Bowl

2000 ROSE BOWL

January 1, 2000, Pasadena, California
Wisconsin 17, Stanford 9

The Badgers were on a mission, from the start of the season, to become the first Big Ten team to win back-to-back Rose Bowls. They accomplished that goal despite an offense that was a bit rusty in the Rose Bowl game, capping off the most incredible decade in school history in terrific fashion.

They accomplished the repeat as heavy favorites, a new role after winning their previous two Rose Bowls as big underdogs. "As a team, it's tough coming out here, being here for a week and hearing all week you're the favorite," Wisconsin redshirt freshman quarterback Brooks Bollinger said. "I don't know if our team fell victim to that and started believing that stuff. It's hard to say."

Whether it was that, or the six-week layoff, or a Stanford defense that had the Badgers well-scouted, the Cardinal led 9–3 at halftime. But the Wisconsin offense got rolling in the second half behind senior tailback Ron Dayne, who finished with 200 rushing yards and his second-straight Rose Bowl MVP. Bollinger also had a key fourth-down conversion with a completion to tight end John Sigmund on the clinching touchdown drive, and the defense limited Stanford to minus-5 yards rushing.

"There's nothing like doing something that no one else has done," UW coach Barry Alvarez said of the back-to-back Rose Bowl wins. "You don't get many opportunities like that in a lifetime. That was one of the things I tried to use as motivation for the kids, for them to go out and do it. Just talking about it doesn't get it done. To get out and do it really makes me proud of them."

Nick Davis (left), Wendell Bryant (above) and the Badgers made history with their 17–9 win over Stanford.

"There's nothing like doing something that no one else has done."
—BARRY ALVAREZ, AFTER HIS BADGERS BECAME THE FIRST BIG TEN TEAM TO WIN
BACK-TO-BACK ROSE BOWLS

2000 SUN BOWL
December 29, 2000, El Paso, Texas
Wisconsin 21, UCLA 20

Wisconsin concluded a difficult season, which began with suspension of more than 20 players for violating NCAA rules by accepting discounts in the Shoe Box scandal. The suspensions were handed down by the NCAA a few hours before the opening game. But the Badgers persevered, despite a three-game losing streak to start Big Ten play, and went out in style with a third-straight bowl victory over the Bruins.

After falling behind 20–7 midway through the third quarter, the Badgers came storming back with a short touchdown pass from Brooks Bollinger to Chris Chambers, set up by Michael Bennett's 54-yard kickoff return.

Ben Herbert made a key fourth-down stop on a fake field goal, and Bollinger drove the offense 70 yards for the go-ahead score, a 6-yard run by Bennett. The Wisconsin defense then made three straight stops, with Jamar Fletcher's interception in the final minute clinching the win.

2002 ALAMO BOWL
December 28, 2002, San Antonio, Texas
Wisconsin 31, Colorado 28, overtime

Barry Alvarez improved to 7–1 in bowl games with another come-from-behind victory against a favored opponent. Playing in his final game, UW senior Brooks Bollinger, the winningest quarterback in school history, made his 30th career victory a memorable one.

The Badgers had been criticized for qualifying for a bowl with a 7–6 record and were seven-point underdogs against the 14th-ranked Buffaloes, but the defense held Colorado to 200 total yards.

With Wisconsin trailing 28–21, Bollinger drove the Badgers 80 yards in 10 plays, twice overcoming lengthy fourth-down situations with clutch completions, scoring the tying touchdown on a one-yard run with 51 seconds remaining in regulation. Bollinger had a 27-yard completion to Brandon Williams on fourth-and-18 and a 28-yard completion to a leaping Darrin Charles on fourth-and-10 to the 1-yard line.

After Colorado missed a field-goal attempt following its overtime possession, Mike Allen booted the game-winner from 37 yards, giving Bollinger the ninth fourth-quarter comeback of his career.

Alvarez's winning percentage of .875 in bowl games at that time trailed only John Robinson, who was 8–1 (.889) at Southern California and UNLV.

"There were a lot of chances for this team to cash it in, say, 'Well, we played hard but we came up short,'" Wisconsin center Al Johnson said. "But they didn't do that. They kept fighting to the end. It just shows the character of the guys on this team."

2006 CAPITAL ONE BOWL
January 1, 2006, Orlando, Florida
Wisconsin 24, Auburn 10

Barry Alvarez re-established his reputation as the bowl master, once and forever, in his final game as Badger head coach. It couldn't have come against a better opponent, either. Auburn was ranked No. 7 and felt it should have been selected for a Bowl Championship Series game.

After losing three bowl games to SEC opponents, the only blemishes on Alvarez's bowl record, the Badgers, who were 10½-point underdogs, gave their coach the perfect parting gift. This was an upset every bit as big as Wisconsin's first two Rose Bowl victories under Alvarez, who set the tone from the start of bowl practices.

"From the very first time we talked to the team, I wanted them to understand we had a chance to win this football game if we played well," Alvarez said. "It didn't make any difference what anyone else said or what the line was, the fact some people didn't think we deserved to be in this game. We'd have a great game plan, and we were talented enough to come in here and win the football game."

After hearing for so long about the SEC's decided advantage in speed, one of the most satisfying things for Alvarez—who always

disputed that argument—was the comment Auburn coach Tommy Tuberville made after the game about the speed of Badger tailback Brian Calhoun (213 rushing yards) and wide receiver Brandon Williams (173 receiving yards) giving his team fits.

"At times, we were in space trying to tackle both of those guys," Tuberville said. "Looking at all the film I looked at over the last month, not many people have tackled them in the open field."

Quarterback John Stocco capped his season of great improvement by throwing for 301 yards and two touchdowns as the Badgers rolled up 548 total yards. UW's much-maligned defense played its best game of the season, holding the SEC's top offense to only one touchdown early in the fourth quarter and 236 total yards, setting the tone by forcing turnovers on the Tigers' first two drives.

Beyond the bowl success, Alvarez wanted something else to stand as his legacy. "You can talk about buildings, you can talk about bowl victories," he said. "I think maybe the thing I'm most proud of is we brought pride back to our fans, for our football program."

"You can talk about buildings, you can talk about bowl victories. I think maybe the thing I'm most proud of is we brought pride back to our fans, for our football program."

—**BARRY ALVAREZ, FOLLOWING HIS FINAL GAME**

2007 CAPITAL ONE BOWL

January 1, 2007, Orlando, Florida
Wisconsin 17, Arkansas 14

The Badgers were shut out of Bowl Championship Series consideration, despite ranking seventh in the final BCS standings, due to a little-discussed rule not allowing more than two teams from the same conference in the same year. With Ohio State playing in the national title game and Michigan in the Rose Bowl, it sent the Badgers back to Orlando for a second straight year.

Arkansas came into the game with the nation's fourth-ranked rushing attack and the Heisman Trophy runner-up in sophomore Darren McFadden. But it was sophomore Felix Jones who did the most damage, rushing for 150 yards on 14 carries as the Razorbacks rolled up 232 rushing yards. The Badgers were held to minus-5 rushing yards, in part due to six sacks of quarterback John Stocco.

But as a sign of how the offense evolved the last two years, UW turned to its much-improved passing game. Stocco threw for 171 yards and two touchdowns in the first half, and the defense wouldn't crack in the second half, when the offense had five-straight three-and-outs.

It was the Badgers' first win of the season over a ranked opponent, although Stocco thought it was hogwash that some critics thought they needed the win over the 12th-ranked Hogs to "validate" their season. "I'm just so tired of hearing that stuff," Stocco said. "You hear it every year. We go out and beat Auburn last year, and everyone says they didn't come out to play. We didn't need to beat this team to validate to us that we're a great team."

"You hear it every year. We go out and beat Auburn last year, and everyone says they didn't come out to play. We didn't need to beat this team to validate to us that we're a great team."

—JOHN STOCCO

GREAT GAMES

October 31, 1942
Camp Randall Stadium
Wisconsin 17, Ohio State 7

Fans didn't pay much attention to rankings back then, and it's doubtful many people in the stands that day knew—or even cared—that Ohio State was ranked No. 1 in the country. In Columbus, Ohio, Buckeyes coach Paul Brown told writers the rankings were "generally classified as a silly type of thing by the men who play the game and know the score." How could writers from different parts of the country rate teams they had never seen play?

The fact the Badgers were playing Ohio State, a team they had not beaten since 1918, was enough for them. It was the most anticipated game of a memorable season, shown by NBC to a national television audience and played by young men who knew they would soon be leaving to fight in World War II.

In an interview with *The Columbus Citizen* prior to the game, Wisconsin coach Harry Stuhldreher acknowledged the impact war had on the season. "I keep picturing the boys who are playing for me as they may be a year from now, battling a Jap or a Nazi with a bayonet," Stuhldreher said. "We've always wanted our players tough. Now we want them tougher than ever. And don't think the boys themselves don't realize it. There's a different attitude this fall over anything I've ever seen either as a player or coach."

On a field filled with a host of stars, Wisconsin's Elroy Hirsch shone brightest. He gained 118 yards rushing on only 13 carries and also had a key 14-yard touchdown pass to end Dave Schreiner for the Badgers' final touchdown. "He was the outstanding back on the field today, one of the best I've ever seen," Brown said after the game. "He makes their whole offense move because he's a touchdown threat every time he has the ball."

October 13, 1951
Camp Randall Stadium
Wisconsin 6, Ohio State 6

Some people regarded Ohio State halfback Vic Janowicz, the 1950 Heisman Trophy winner, as possibly the greatest Buckeye of all time. Almost nobody could stop Janowicz—until, that is, he ran into the Wisconsin defense known as the "Hard Rocks."

The Wisconsin defense was so formidable that season, it scored more points (58) than it allowed (53). Against that unit, Janowicz didn't stand a chance, finishing with 11 net yards on 11 carries. He also missed the extra point that could have broken the tie in the fourth quarter in front of a record crowd of 51,156.

However, Janowicz's average of 43.8 punting yards helped keep the Wisconsin offense contained, and the Badgers settled for the tie, despite a 19–7 edge in first downs and a 346–106 advantage in total yards.

November 10, 1962
Camp Randall Stadium
Wisconsin 37, Northwestern 6

Of all the memories Pat Richter has from his great career at Wisconsin, this game stands out as one of the best. Northwestern, coached by the legendary Ara Parseghian, was ranked No. 1 and had a heralded quarterback-receiver combination in Tom Myers and Paul Flatley. Myers led the Big Ten in passing.

But the Badgers, who were headed to the Rose Bowl that season, had a pretty good combination of their own in Ron Vander Kelen and Richter. Vander Kelen, who also could run, ranked No. 1 in the Big Ten in total offense and No. 2 in passing. Flatley and Richter were one-two in the conference in receptions.

It turned out the Wisconsin offense, helped by running back Louis Holland, had too much balance for the Wildcats. Holland scored three touchdowns, including two on the ground. Vander Kelen threw for 181 yards and three scores, compared to 181 yards and one score for Myers. Richter caught five passes for 77 yards, while Flatley had only two catches for 17 yards.

October 11, 1969
Camp Randall Stadium
Wisconsin 23, Iowa 17

With anti-war protests raging and losses piling up under coach John Coatta, the football program took a back seat on campus. The Badgers went through 23 games without a victory, and the only pause to the steady drumbeat of losing was a 21–21 tie against Iowa in Coatta's first year in 1967.

Going into the 1969 season, there was hope the misery would end, but Wisconsin lost its first three games, all at home. It didn't look any better the following week, when the Hawkeyes led 17–0 in the third quarter. Then, a miracle happened. The Badgers scored 23 straight points behind quarterback Neil Graff, who threw a 17-yard touchdown pass to Randy Marks on fourth-and-11 for the go-ahead touchdown.

For the first time in 1,057 days, the Badgers won a football game. The fans, who couldn't control themselves, stormed onto the field— with more than a minute left in the game. After they were ushered back to the sidelines, the clock ran out and the postgame celebration quickly moved up State Street. A *Wisconsin State Journal* reporter compared the scene, with thousands of delirious fans, to old movies of the American liberation of Paris.

September 21, 1974
Camp Randall Stadium
Wisconsin 21, Nebraska 20

Wisconsin set the stage for this upset by playing well in a 20–16 loss in Lincoln, Nebraska, the year before against a Cornhuskers team coming off back-to-back national championships. So, the Badgers were feeling pretty good about themselves going into the rematch.

Still, fourth-ranked Nebraska led 17–14 in the fourth quarter, with the help of four Badger turnovers, including two fumbles by running back Billy Marek and two interceptions thrown by quarterback Gregg Bohlig.

After 10 straight running plays, the Cornhuskers had a first-and-goal at the UW 2-yard line and seemed poised to put the game away. But the Wisconsin defense rose up for a stirring goal-line stand, stopping three straight running plays and forcing a field goal that made it 20–14.

Following a first-down sack on the next series, Bohlig rolled to his right, behind his two running backs for extra protection, and heaved a deep pass to Jeff Mack. Nebraska safety George Kyros, who had an earlier interception, went after another one and ended up interfering with Mack, who made the catch anyway and completed the 77-yard scoring play.

Wisconsin cracked the national rankings for the first time in 10 years, rocketing up to No. 11 in the Associated Press poll. Coach John Jardine said it signaled a turnaround, and his team finished 7–4 that season. It was the Badgers' only winning season in Jardine's eight years, and he resigned under pressure three years later.

September 12, 1981
Camp Randall Stadium
Wisconsin 21, Michigan 14

In the Wolverines' 24–0 victory in Madison the previous year, coach Bo Schembechler had taken part in a little gamesmanship with the UW fans. Late in the third quarter, Michigan had a fourth-and-1 at the Badgers' 4-yard line, in front of the UW student section.

With the crowd roaring, quarterback John Wangler stepped up to the line seven times and each time—under strict orders from Schembechler—he backed away from center, complaining his teammates couldn't hear because of the deafening noise. Referee Glen Fortin warned the Badgers twice, then stripped them of all their timeouts. That was followed by two delay-of-game penalties, the first of which gave the Wolverines a first down, and they eventually scored. Following the game, Schembechler talked about the lack of sophistication among Wisconsin fans.

The next year, in the season opener, the Badgers were ready. They dominated the game statistically, with a 23–8 edge in first downs. Michigan got 89 yards on one play, a touchdown run by Butch Woolfolk in the third quarter that made it 14–14, and were still outgained 439–229.

Wisconsin answered Woolfolk's run, springing tailback John Williams for a 71-yard touchdown on a screen pass and a 21–14 lead. Michigan had all of the fourth quarter remaining but quarterback Steve Smith, making his first start, threw three interceptions to safety Matt VandenBoom on the final six possessions.

October 23, 1982
Camp Randall Stadium
Illinois 29, Wisconsin 28

This much is remembered: Receiver Al Toon fielded a "bounce pass" from quarterback Randy Wright, then threw a perfect 40-yard scoring pass to tight end Jeff Nault to put the Badgers ahead with 52 seconds remaining.

This is sometimes forgotten: The Badgers botched the extra point, one of two they missed in the game, leaving their lead at 28–26. Illini quarterback Tony Eason, who threw for 479 yards in the game, coolly drove his team into field-goal position, and rotund kicker Mike Bass booted a 46-yard field goal, his fifth of the game, leaving the Badgers with a gut-wrenching loss.

Still, the "bounce pass"—it was actually a one-hop lateral to Toon, behind the line of scrimmage—became one of the most famous plays in Badger history. The throw to Toon was meant to get the defenders to relax, thinking it was an incomplete pass, and it worked to perfection. "It was so pretty, that I didn't even look downfield," Illinois coach Mike White said. "I just knew it was disaster."

October 30, 1993
Camp Randall Stadium
Wisconsin 13, Michigan 10

What should have been a glorious postgame celebration after a victory that stamped the Badgers as legitimate Rose Bowl contenders, turned terrifying in a matter of seconds when students tried to storm the field, trampling people in the front rows.

Walk-on Rick Schnetzky booted two field goals in his first significant action, and Terrell Fletcher scored on a 12-yard run late in the first half to stake the Badgers to a 13–3 halftime lead. Then the defense took over, including an interception by cornerback Jeff

Messenger and a fourth-down stop to halt two Michigan drives.

An estimated 12,000 students in the northeast corner of the stadium surged toward the field at the end of the game, crushing people in the front row against a three-foot-high railing, which was pulled from its concrete moorings by the force of the crowd. The next barrier was a chain-link fence surrounding the field. The people who couldn't scramble over the fence got pinned against it.

At least 70 people were taken to hospitals, including seven with critical injuries. Amazingly, nobody died, thanks in large part to the efforts of several UW players who worked to free those who were trapped in the tangle of bodies.

Mike Brin, Joe Panos, Tyler Adam, Brent Moss, John Hall and Brian Patterson were publicly recognized for their heroic efforts.

"I've never had a peak and valley like that," a red-eyed Panos, an offensive tackle and team captain, said after the game. "The win right now means nothing to me, to be honest with you. It's good for the team and all that, but all I care about is to make sure that those people are all right."

December 4, 1993, Tokyo Dome
Wisconsin 41, Michigan State 20

It seemed like a good idea at the time. With the Athletic Department in debt and attendance at home football games declining, Wisconsin officials in May 1992 decided to move a home game against Michigan State to Tokyo to become the first Big Ten teams to play in the Coca-Cola Bowl. Each team earned $400,000, plus travel expenses.

But when the Badgers surprised everybody that season and climbed into Big Ten title contention, needing only to beat the Spartans to go to their first Rose Bowl in 31 years, the decision to give up a home game looked like it might backfire in a big way.

Instead, it just added another interesting twist and backdrop to an unforgettable season.

The Spartans took an early 7–3 lead, but the Badgers gained control with three second-quarter touchdowns. Running back Brent Moss rushed for 147 yards, his 10th-straight game with more than 100 yards, and Terrell Fletcher joined him with 112. Wide receiver Lee DeRamus caught five passes for 96 yards, tying Al Toon's school single-season record for receptions (54) and surpassing him in yards (920).

"This was the greatest going from the outhouse to the penthouse as quick as we did," said coach Barry Alvarez, whose team won one game in his first year in 1990.

October 11, 2003
Camp Randall Stadium
Wisconsin 17, Ohio State 10

There's something about the lights that seems to bring out the best in the Badgers. Seldom-used backup quarterback Matt Schabert took over for the injured Jim Sorgi and completed a 79-yard touchdown pass to Lee Evans for the winning touchdown with 5:20 remaining in the game against the defending national champions.

The win was the 15th in the past 16 night games for Wisconsin and improved its record to 16–5 under the lights in coach Barry Alvarez's 14 seasons at the time. It also snapped a 19-game winning streak by No. 3 Ohio State.

Sorgi was knocked out of the game when he was choked in a pile by Buckeyes linebacker Robert Reynolds. Schabert's only other extensive playing time came in a loss to Michigan State two years earlier. But he was ready when called upon, completing two passes for 104 yards and also running for a key first down on a bootleg.

Schabert later transferred, prior to his senior season, due to a lack of playing time. But he left his mark in a big way, despite his limited chances. "Matt Schabert stepped in, in a tough situation," UW coach Barry Alvarez said. "Boy, did Schabert do a job."

Camp Randall rocked during and after Wisconsin's 17–10 win over Ohio State in 2003.

Erasmus James carries one of the most storied trophies in college football: Paul Bunyan's Axe, emblematic of a Wisconsin win over Minnesota.

The Rivalries

Some great rivalries have helped define Wisconsin football and have given fans many of their greatest memories. One of those rivalries just happens to boast the most distinctive trophy in all of college football.

WISCONSIN–MINNESOTA

It causes grown men to act like children, and it can reduce the toughest of football players to tears. That's the power of Paul Bunyan's Axe, the trophy given annually to the winner of the most-played rivalry in NCAA Division I-A football, between Wisconsin and Minnesota.

Scott Starks, a cornerback for the Badgers from 2001 to 2004, has witnessed the power of the Axe up close and seen the effect it can have on players who come to possess it following hard-fought games.

"When people get the Axe, they turn into totally different people," Starks said. "They're like little kids, chopping down goal posts, people riding on it. … But if you ever get a chance to do it, it's just an amazing feeling."

Wisconsin and Minnesota first met in 1890 and have faced each other every year since 1907—116 games and counting through 2006, one game more than Missouri-Kansas. The 1906 game was canceled by President Theodore Roosevelt, who wanted to cool off heated college football rivalries due to injuries and deaths on the field.

In 1914 Minnesota played Wisconsin in the Golden Gophers' first homecoming game. The Badgers' first homecoming was against Minnesota in 1919. Between the years 1923 and 1925, the two teams played to three straight ties.

To capture the atmosphere surrounding the rivalry, Dr. R.B. Fouch of Minneapolis fashioned a bacon slab out of black walnut, to serve as a traveling trophy, which he hoped would compare to the "Little Brown Jug," which Minnesota and Michigan played for every year.

The "Slab of Bacon," first played for in 1930, had a football carved on top, inscribed with an "M" or a "W," depending on which way you held it. The idea was that the winning team "got to bring home the bacon." It was to be presented to the winning school by a sorority from the losing institution.

The Gophers dominated the series—and everybody else—in the 1930s, winning nine straight games from 1933 to 1941 under legendary coach Bernie Bierman. After taking over in 1932, Bierman led Minnesota to seven Big Ten championships and five national championships over the next 10 years, the so-called, "Golden Decade."

The "Slab of Bacon" went missing in the early 1940s. The Wisconsin version of the story is that the trophy was discontinued. The Minnesota version has to do with a melee on the field following one game and Wisconsin's failure to make the presentation to the winners. The trophy was eventually found in a storage room at Camp Randall Stadium during a cleanup project, which caused Wisconsin coach Barry Alvarez in 1992 to crow, "We took home the bacon and kept it."

Since a new trophy was needed, The National W Club, Wisconsin's letterwinners' club, came up with the Axe, first presented to Minnesota, 16–0 winners in 1948. The score of the first game in the series, a 63–0 Minnesota victory in 1890—the fourth game ever played by the Badgers—is printed on the six-foot handle near the Axe's head. The results of every successive game line the handle in red ink.

The rivalry went on for so long that in the 1960s, the scores started getting smaller and smaller, scrunching the letters to save room. The original Axe was donated to the College Football Hall of Fame in South Bend, Indiana, by the two schools. The 56-year-old trophy was becoming unstable, due in part to postgame celebrations by the winning school, and the handle was running out of room for scores. A sturdier Axe was created in 2000 by the W Club.

The Axe itself didn't play a prominent role in the rivalry until Alvarez arrived at Wisconsin in 1990, and the coaches on both sides started playing up the significance of the trophy. Alvarez started a tradition of having Jim Hueber, a former Gophers assistant who joined the staff in 1992, talk to the players at the start of the week of the Minnesota game, about the long and colorful history of rivalry.

"He loved doing that," said Joe Stellmacher, a safety with the Badgers from 2002 to 2006. "He had all sorts of crazy stories. That was really his thing."

One of the stories had to do with Francis "Pug" Lund, the former Minnesota All-American halfback, from Rice Lake, Wisconsin, who played from 1932 to 1934 and suffered a broken finger that did not set properly and left it protruding at an awkward angle.

As legend has it, Lund had the doctor surgically remove the tip of his finger.

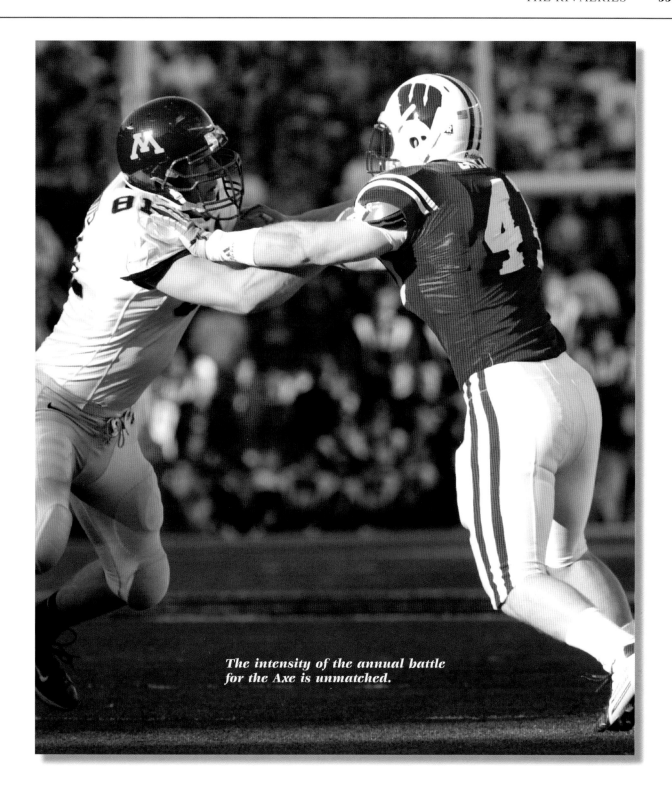

*The intensity of the annual battle
for the Axe is unmatched.*

"This team needed this. *The young players needed it extremely badly so they can carry on. The older guys needed it because they want to leave a legacy. It's awful nice that for once we're going home, and we're going to be able to enjoy the trip home."*

—ALVAREZ AFTER SNAPPING A 23-GAME ROAD LOSING STREAK, AND 19-GAME CONFERENCE LOSING STREAK, WITH A 19–16 VICTORY AT MINNESOTA ON NOVEMBER 14, 1992.

"His quote supposedly was, 'Better to lose a finger than fumble a football,'" Alvarez said.

The two teams also produced some memorable games in the 1960s. The Badgers intercepted three passes and upset the third-ranked Gophers 23–21 in 1961, the Gophers' only conference defeat, which cost them a share of the title.

Wisconsin was ranked No. 3 in 1962 and playing for a spot in the Rose Bowl when it defeated No. 5 Minnesota, 14–9, with Ralph Kurek scoring the winning touchdown with 1:37 remaining.

It's not the Axe itself, of course, but the history it stands for that makes it significant. "The true focus is actually on the game," Minnesota coach Glen Mason said. "I've said many, many times—obviously, I didn't create this rivalry. Neither did Barry Alvarez. We're just charged with carrying it on.

"There's history behind it. It's more than just two teams or two schools, it's two states, and sometimes there is even deeper meaning than that."

There was also something about these two teams that produced wild and unpredictable games when they met, especially in the Metrodome.

One of Alvarez's strongest memories of his trips to the Metrodome will always be his first one in 1991, his first road victory at UW and first conference win. Badger safety Melvin Tucker secured the 19–16 victory with a jarring hit in the end zone on a fourth-down pass to knock the ball loose from tight end Patt Evans.

Hueber remembered the game for a different reason. He was on the Minnesota sideline, in his eighth season as an assistant coach with the Gophers. The staff got fired the next day.

Alvarez will forever be haunted by the 1993 loss in the Metrodome, which may have cost his team the national championship. Wisconsin came into the game with a 6–0 record, and quarterback Darrell Bevell threw for a school-record 423 yards as part of 605 yards of total offense. But Bevell, who had thrown only four interceptions in the first six games, was picked off five times as the 14-point underdog Gophers pulled out a 28–21 win.

Minnesota went on to finish 4–7, while the Badgers went 10–1–1, tying Ohio State, and winning their first Rose Bowl under Alvarez to finish No. 6 in the country. "Had we won that football game...we would have been the only team in the country that was undefeated," Alvarez said.

Alvarez missed the 1999 game in the Metrodome, watching on TV from his hospital bed 75 miles away at the Mayo Clinic in Rochester, Minnesota, following knee-replacement surgery. UW defensive line coach John Palermo filled in for Alvarez, and Vitaly Pisetsky's 31-yard field goal lifted UW to a 20–17 victory in its first overtime game.

But even that couldn't top the finish in Alvarez's final game in the Metrodome as head coach in 2005. Freshman linebacker Jonathan Casillas blocked a punt that was recovered in the end zone for the winning touchdown by Ben Strickland with 30 seconds remaining in the Badgers' 38–34 victory.

Perhaps the best thing about the rivalry in recent years is that the emotion never spilled over into ugly incidents. "I think we're both proud that you see good, clean football played, and you haven't seen some of those antics that you see at some other schools where you have the fights and the planting of the flag and all that stuff that's really not good for college football," Mason said.

Alvarez had a trophy case built for the Axe, and when the case stands empty, like it was following a heartbreaking 37–34 loss in the Metrodome in 2003, reclaiming it takes on added significance the following year.

"That's our emphasis," Alvarez said in 2004. "That's one way you can really focus on this football game. It's a tremendous rivalry. We'll show them all the clips of former years. We've already given them their history lesson on the Axe and the rivalry.

"We'll make it important, because it is important, just a part of college football history, the longest ongoing rivalry. I think it's important for the guys to know that. We build a trophy case for that Axe and it's empty. That's not good."

In addition to the talk from Hueber, Alvarez had a videotape continually running in the locker room, showing past celebrations with the Axe following victories over Minnesota.

They were always the same. The team in possession of the Axe, having won it the year before, always put it in a safe location near the bench. Then, as the final seconds ticked off the clock, players on the winning team positioned themselves to be the first one to grab the Axe.

What followed was a euphoric parade around the field by the winning team, with players taking turns holding the Axe—always stopping to pretend to cut down the goalposts. As silly as it sounds, the players take it seriously.

"When we won the Axe...it was a great feeling," said Wisconsin defensive tackle Anttaj Hawthorne, who played from 2001 to 2004. "It's kind of hard to explain the feeling. It's real emotional, you know that you worked hard for it. Parading around the field with the Axe is probably the best thing."

And losing the Axe is certainly the worst thing, especially when it has been in one team's possession and the opposing team comes racing to its bench to pick it up.

"That's just a sick feeling, to see another team run over there and just violate your sideline and take something that's been inside your locker room for a year," Starks said. "That's a bad feeling."

Mike Samuel

WISCONSIN–IOWA

When Bret Bielema became the defensive coordinator at Wisconsin in 2004, before taking over as head coach in 2006, he liked to joke that he arrived with two strikes against him. "I was born in Illinois and I played at Iowa," Bielema said.

Bielema grew up in Prophetstown, Illinois, on a hog farm, then walked on at Iowa, where he earned four letters, from 1989 to 1992. He was a member of Iowa's Big Ten championship team in 1990, a starting nose guard as a junior in 1991 and a team co-captain as a senior.

Truth be told, of those two strikes, there is no doubt the Iowa part of his heritage caused Wisconsin fans the most angst. Part of it had to do with the fact that Bielema had a tattoo of an Iowa Tiger Hawk on one calf, which some fans found particularly galling.

The preoccupation with Bielema's Iowa roots got so bad that during contract negotiations prior to his taking over as head coach in December 2005, he was forced to confront an Internet rumor that he had an out clause in his contract to go to Iowa. No such clause existed and was never part of any contract discussions, according to both Bielema and Alvarez.

Despite assuring fans his heart was solely with the Badgers, the tattoo issue wouldn't go away. Such is the depth of the rivalry between Iowa and Wisconsin. Minnesota is the Badgers' oldest rival, but Iowa is the most hated by fans. In this case, familiarity did breed contempt, and the 1990 hiring of Alvarez, a former Hawkeyes assistant, only added to the depth of those feelings.

Alvarez got his first college coaching job under Hayden Fry at Iowa in 1979 and spent eight seasons as an assistant coach in Iowa City, Iowa. When it came time for Alvarez to handpick his successor, he chose Bielema, whose ties to Iowa ran even deeper, including his playing days.

When Bielema's playing career was over, Fry helped convince him to go into coaching and hired him, first as a graduate assistant in 1994, then as a full-time linebackers coach two years later. Kirk Ferentz succeeded Fry in 1999, and Bielema was one of two assistant coaches who were retained. Even when Bielema ventured away from Iowa, to become the co-defensive coordinator and linebackers coach at Kansas State in 2002 and 2003, it was under Bill Snyder, another branch of the Fry coaching tree.

Wisconsin and Iowa had similar playing styles and philosophies. They recruited many of the same players. "Our programs are built around the same fundamentals, and anytime Iowa and Wisconsin are going to play, it is going to be a dogfight," Wisconsin offensive lineman Joe Thomas said.

Joe Panos grabs a Hawkeye.

Bielema was asked constantly about his Iowa roots after taking over as head coach in 2006. "You cannot change who you are or where you came from," he said. "It makes you who you are today. If you ever lose sight of that, you'll never be somewhere for a long period of time."

Despite proud histories, both programs endured bleak stretches in the late 1960s.

When the Badgers had a 23-game stretch without a victory from 1967 to 1969, the only reprieve was a 21–21 tie against the Hawkeyes in 1967. When Wisconsin's misery finally ended in 1969, the relief came via a 23–17 victory over Iowa.

The Hawkeyes ended two decades of misery in 1979 with the hiring of Fry, who would lead them to two Rose Bowls. Fry won his first game against the Badgers, 24–13, which was Iowa's third straight win in the series and a sign of things to come.

In one of the most exasperating streaks in UW history, the Badgers went 0–17–1 against Iowa from 1977 to 1996. Even the arrival of Alvarez, the Fry disciple, couldn't seem to turn the tide.

"It's great to keep our unbeaten streak against Wisconsin alive," Fry said following a 31–0 pounding of the Badgers in 1996, which improved his record to 5–0 against Alvarez. "I've never lost to one of my former assistant coaches and didn't want for it to happen today."

The Badgers finally exorcised those demons with a 13–10 upset of Iowa in front of a frenzied crowd at Camp Randall Stadium in 1997. "You guys cannot understand how badly we wanted this game," senior cornerback LaMar Campbell told reporters afterward. "Not many people get to see how emotional that locker room was. I think we would have killed and died for each other out there, and that's a great feeling to play with guys you know feel that way."

While Fry lost his last two games against the Badgers to finish with a 15–2–1 record against them, it might have been a small price for Wisconsin to pay, given that two of his coaching protégés eventually became head coaches at the school.

One of the best things Bielema could have done to endear himself to Badger fans his first year—and make them forget about that tattoo—was beat Iowa. That was something Bielema acknowledged before the 2006 season, after being part of losses to the Hawkeyes as the defensive coordinator the previous two years. The worst was the 30–7 loss in Kinnick Stadium in 2004 that knocked Wisconsin out of the Rose Bowl.

"I think back all the time to all the great experiences I've had, the great people I've been able to be around...first and foremost Hayden Fry," Bielema said. "He gave me my scholarship, which helped my checkbook a lot, then gave me my first job.

"I have a lot of respect and admiration for him. Now, within the conference, the University of Wisconsin and Iowa are probably very similar from a program standpoint. I know what the (losing) end of the last two games has been (like), so I'm trying to revert that (trend) in a hurry."

Bielema went out and accomplished that in his first attempt, a 24–21 victory over Iowa that was part of a sterling 11–1 regular-season in his first year. Suddenly, the tattoo no longer seemed like such a big deal.

"I think we would have killed and died for each other out there, and that's a great feeling to play with guys you know feel that way."

—CORNERBACK LAMAR CAMPBELL, FOLLOWING WISCONSIN'S 13–10 WIN OVER IOWA IN 1997

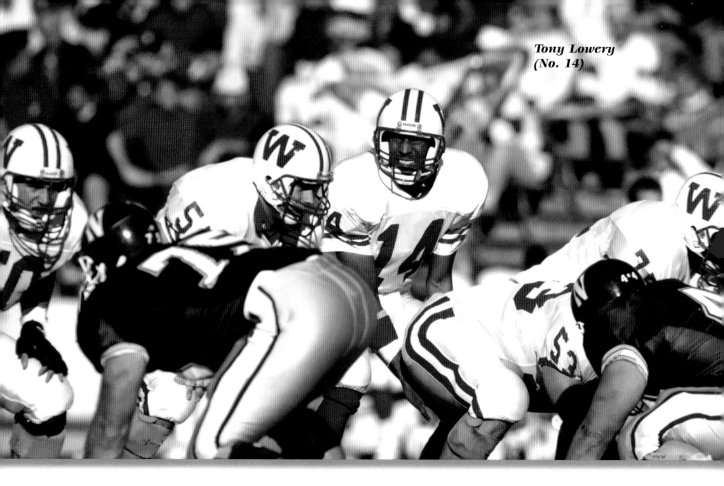

WISCONSIN–NORTHWESTERN

When assessing Wisconsin's biggest rivals, Northwestern does not come immediately to mind. The Wildcats are not one of the two "protected" teams for the Badgers—that status belongs to Minnesota and Iowa—meaning that every few years, Northwestern drops off the schedule for two years.

The two teams do not play for a trophy, like many of college football's more celebrated rivalries.

The series has had long stretches where it was one-sided, mostly in favor of UW. From 1891 to 1921, the Badgers were 14–0–4. From 1949 to 1963, they were 13–2. They also won 13 straight from 1972 to 1984. The best stretch for the Wildcats was going 5–0–1 from 1966 to 1971.

Still, there are some factors that make this a legitimate rivalry. One is history. It's the second-oldest current rivalry for the Badgers, who played their first game against Northwestern in 1890, losing 22–10. It came in their second season of football and less than two weeks after their first game against Minnesota.

Another thing is proximity. Evanston, Illinois, is approximately 150 miles from Madison, making it the closest Big Ten campus. Toss in the natural Wisconsin-Illinois bitterness, and it has all the necessary ingredients for a good rivalry.

Those feelings escalated when Barry Alvarez was hired at Wisconsin in 1990 and Gary Barnett came along two years later at Northwestern. Both coaches took over downtrodden programs and took them places almost nobody else thought they could go.

Wisconsin shocked Big Ten followers with the first of three titles and Rose Bowl victories under Alvarez during his fourth season in 1993. Northwestern shocked many of the same people with a Big Ten title and Rose Bowl appearance during the 1995 season, in Barnett's fourth year.

Also, Alvarez and Barnett were not close. There were bad feelings that reportedly started in their first meeting in 1992, which Northwestern won 27–25 to end the Badgers' bowl hopes. The two programs also competed hard for many of the same recruits.

The two teams played some wild games during that time, which added to the intensity. The Wildcats won 34–30 in 1996 at Camp Randall Stadium in the infamous "take-a-knee game." After Northwestern missed a 55-yard field-goal attempt, the Badgers had the ball at their own 38-yard line with 1:33 remaining.

Alvarez determined it was too much time to have his quarterback take a knee and tried to run out the clock, but freshman tailback Ron Dayne fumbled a handoff from Mike Samuel. The Wildcats recovered and scored the winning touchdown with 37 seconds left.

The next year, the Badgers prevailed 26–25 at Ryan Field on a last-second field goal by Matt Davenport.

But that was nothing compared to the 2000 meeting, which might go down as the most entertaining in series history. The Badgers played this game without six players

suspended for receiving improper benefits from an area shoe store, but they led 23–14 midway through the third quarter at home against the Wildcats. Then the roof caved in.

Northwestern was taking the conference by storm with a newfangled, no-huddle spread offense. When the last pass had finally been thrown, Northwestern had piled up 544 yards of offense in a 47–44 double-overtime victory. Prior to that game, the Badgers had been 100–0 when scoring 40 or more points. They lost despite a 293-yard rushing performance by Michael Bennett. While Northwestern went on to win a share of the conference title, the Badgers lost their next two games before recovering to finish 9–4, winning the Sun Bowl against UCLA, with what Alvarez often said was his most talented team.

That game was a precursor to another wild battle in 2005, when the Wildcats won 51–48 and finished with a staggering 674 total yards, the most ever allowed in a game by UW.

The simmering rivalry boiled over in the final seconds in 1999, as the Badgers' 35–19 victory in Evanston was winding down. There were personal foul penalties on both sides, punches were thrown on the last play and there were heated words exchanged between the coaching staffs as they exited the press box.

That prompted second-year Northwestern coach Randy Walker to say, "I think all of us know, it's a great rivalry. It's one of the best in college football."

WISCONSIN–MICHIGAN

It takes two sides to make a rivalry, which means this one was one short for many years. Also, Michigan players would probably scoff at the notion the Badgers had risen from the level of occasional nuisance to legitimate rival.

Yet, at least from the perspective of the Wisconsin players and fans, there is something undeniably special about the Michigan game. The Badgers have used that game as a barometer of sorts for measuring the status of their own program.

When the Badgers ended an 18-year streak without a bowl game in 1981, it was a 21–14 victory over top-ranked Michigan in the opener that turned them into believers.

When the Badgers went to the 1994 Rose Bowl, it was a 13–10 victory over Michigan that stamped them as legitimate contenders.

Still, UW has known mostly suffering at the hands of the Wolverines for most of the series. From 1965 until 1990, Wisconsin lost 23 of 24 games. Despite back-to-back wins in 1993 and 1994 by the Badgers, Alvarez managed just a 3–7 record against Michigan, a .300 winning percentage that was his worst against Big Ten opponents.

It included six straight losses, many in agonizing fashion, like the 20–17 loss at home in 2001, in which a Michigan punt in the final seconds bounced off the back of the leg of UW freshman defensive back Brett Bell and led to the game-winning field goal.

But Alvarez managed to go out on a high note against Michigan with a thrilling 23–20 victory in 2005 in front of a frenzied crowd of 83,022, the second-largest at the time at Camp Randall Stadium. John Stocco scored the winning touchdown on a four-yard run on a quarterback draw with 24 seconds to play.

"I think that was probably the most unbelievable atmosphere I've ever been in, in my life," Stocco said. "The fans are unbelievable. I couldn't believe how loud it was. It's just great to do this for Coach. I know he hasn't had a lot of success against those guys in the past, and he's done nothing but good things for us. I'm really happy for him."

Casey Rabach springs Brooks Bollinger with a pancake of a Wolverine.

Talkin' Badger Football

We thought we'd go straight to the source and let some of Wisconsin's greatest legends—and others with a unique perspective—share their thoughts about Badger football. They put it much better than we could.

"Most of us will be in there with you boys in a short while, and the season has certainly helped to get us in shape for the days to come."

— ALL-AMERICA END DAVE SCHREINER IN A LETTER DURING THE 1942 SEASON TO FORMER BADGERS SERVING IN THE MILITARY DURING WORLD WAR II. SCHREINER LATER DIED FIGHTING ON OKINAWA.

"I learned a great lesson this year. I don't care how much talent you have, if you make mistakes you're not going to win ballgames. I don't care who you are playing."

— LINEBACKER JIM MELKA, AFTER 20–19 LOSS TO KENTUCKY ON DECEMBER 29, 1984, IN THE HALL OF FAME BOWL.

"I'm not going to try and paint any rosy pictures. *I don't know how long it's going to take to turn it around. All I can do is get the kids to play as hard as they can. If we can do that, it will be fun."*

—COACH BARRY ALVAREZ AT HIS INTRODUCTORY PRESS CONFERENCE, JANUARY 2, 1990.

"I know we have to start someplace. *We won a game. We beat a (Mid-American Conference) team. But we have a heck of a long way to go."*

—ALVAREZ AFTER HIS FIRST VICTORY, 24–7, OVER BALL STATE ON SEPTEMBER 15, 1990.

"I took a pitchout on the first play of the second half. *It was just a question of going all the way. I could have made it an 80-yard run, but I got caught from behind. Then they stopped us. We didn't even get a field goal out of it. But that's one of those things that haunt you. If I'd have had O.J. Simpson or Jim Brown kind of speed, I'd have been in the end zone. But you do the best with what God gave you."*

—ALAN "THE HORSE" AMECHE, REMINISCING MORE THAN 30 YEARS LATER ABOUT BEING CAUGHT FROM BEHIND ON A 54-YARD RUN EARLY IN THE THIRD QUARTER IN A 7–0 LOSS TO SOUTHERN CALIFORNIA IN THE BADGERS' FIRST ROSE BOWL IN 1953.

"I'm still not very comfortable about the way it happened... *(but) somebody has to coach the Badgers, and I would prefer that be me."*

—INTERIM COACH JIM HILLES IN 1986, AFTER THE DEATH OF DAVE McCLAIN.

Barry Alvarez

Joe Panos, No. 58

"There has never been a more loved and admired ambassador for Badger sports than Elroy Hirsch. His charismatic and charming personality brought smiles to so many Badger fans. Anyone who came in contact with him enjoyed a special treat. He loved life, loved people and loved the Badgers."
— UW ATHLETIC DIRECTOR PAT RICHTER AFTER THE DEATH OF ELROY HIRSCH IN 2004.

"Someone has to win the Big Ten Conference title. It might as well be us."
— OFFENSIVE TACKLE JOE PANOS AFTER A 27–15 WIN OVER INDIANA IN THE 1993 BIG TEN OPENER.

"This elderly gentlemen gets up to testify. He's saying what a terrible thing this is for the university. It should never, ever be considered, much less approved. It's lousy public policy. He's just railing against the university's efforts to sign a contract with Reebok. He gets done testifying, he walks down the aisle. The guy who had just been ripping the university and the athletic department up and down about this contract leans over, says, 'No offense, Pat, that '63 Rose Bowl was the greatest football game I've ever seen.'"
— UW ASSOCIATE ATHLETIC DIRECTOR VINCE SWEENEY ABOUT A HEARING HE ATTENDED WITH ATHLETIC DIRECTOR PAT RICHTER, BEFORE THE BOARD OF REGENTS, CONCERNING THE ATHLETIC DEPARTMENT'S PROPOSED CONTRACT WITH REEBOK, AND THE ENDURING POPULARITY OF THE 1963 ROSE BOWL.

"But this is better, because this is my show, baby. It just feels great."
— ALVAREZ, COMPARING THE FEELING OF GOING TO HIS FIRST ROSE BOWL WITH PLAYING IN MAJOR BOWL GAMES AS AN ASSISTANT COACH AT IOWA AND NOTRE DAME.

"They're as good a team as we've faced all year. *They are very underrated nationally. When you think of the Big Ten, you usually think of Michigan and Ohio State. But you have to recognize that they're the Big Ten champions and when you play that level of competition at their caliber, they deserve a lot of respect."*

—UCLA COACH TERRY DONAHUE ON THE BADGERS, PRIOR TO THE 1994 ROSE BOWL.

"It's like you're a prizefighter. *Undisputed heavyweight champion. That's what we are. We are the top. We are the best, and it feels really, really good to say that."*

—DEFENSIVE TACKLE WENDELL BRYANT AFTER WISCONSIN CLAIMED ITS FIRST UNDISPUTED BIG TEN CONFERENCE TITLE SINCE 1962 WITH A VICTORY OVER IOWA ON NOVEMBER 13, 1999.

"We took the approach that this was our home game. *That's why we were in that (home) locker room. That's why we wore our red jerseys. I told the kids this was our home field, to go out and walk the field beforehand and get comfortable. We play well at home, so I expected them to play well."*

—ALVAREZ FOLLOWING THE 21–16 VICTORY
OVER UCLA IN THE ROSE BOWL ON JANUARY 1, 1994.

"We knew we could win. *That's the first thing that you need. We believed, and we believed in each other. We didn't really care what other people thought. We just believed in each other and played as a team. It came out how we wanted it."*

—CENTER DONOVAN RAIOLA AFTER WISCONSIN'S 17–10 VICTORY
SNAPPED OHIO STATE'S 19-GAME WINNING STREAK ON OCTOBER 11, 2003.

Wendell Bryant

Ron Dayne

"Just going out and being businesslike and not talking a lot of trash and showboating. Just going out and doing your job and getting everything done that you had to get done."

—RON DAYNE, DESCRIBING HIS RUNNING STYLE WHILE ACCEPTING THE HEISMAN TROPHY ON DECEMBER 11, 1999.

"He can overpower you. But then when you think he's going to overpower you, he uses his finesse and makes you miss. I don't think we've seen a running back like that all year."

—UCLA LINEBACKER TONY WHITE AFTER RON DAYNE RUSHED FOR 246 YARDS IN THE 1999 ROSE BOWL.

"He will not understand that until years from now, when he understands the fraternity he's about to join. Some of these people he's rubbing shoulders with now, he'll be able to rub shoulders with the rest of his life. There are some high-powered people here. It's an elite fraternity."

—ALVAREZ, ON DECEMBER 11, 1999, BEFORE RON DAYNE
WAS NAMED THE HEISMAN TROPHY WINNER.

"I felt great five years ago because most of our players were back. I didn't do a very good job of getting the message across to them that they had to stay hungry. We didn't become as good a team as we could have, so I addressed that with our young players as soon as the game was over. I'm not the smartest guy in the world, but I'm not going to let the same thing happen again."

—ALVAREZ ON JANUARY 1, 1999, ABOUT LEARNING
HIS LESSON FROM THE FIRST ROSE BOWL.

"We're blue-collar guys. We're not Madison Avenue by any stretch of the imagination."

—ALVAREZ AFTER A VICTORY OVER ILLINOIS ON OCTOBER 17, 1998.

"I told (the team) before the game, isn't Camp Randall painted up beautifully today?"

—ALVAREZ ON THE ROSE BOWL STADIUM ON JANUARY 1, 1994.

"There's nothing like doing something that no one else has done. You don't get many opportunities like that in a lifetime. That was one of the things I tried to use as motivation for the kids, for them to go out and do it. Just talking about it doesn't get it done. To get out and do it really makes me proud of them."

— ALVAREZ ON BECOMING THE FIRST BIG TEN TEAM TO WIN
BACK-TO-BACK ROSE BOWL TITLES ON JANUARY 2, 2000.

"This may be the longest day I've ever had to go through in coaching."

— ALVAREZ AFTER 26 PLAYERS WERE SUSPENDED JUST HOURS BEFORE THE
OPENING GAME AGAINST WESTERN MICHIGAN ON AUGUST 31, 2000.

"We accomplished a lot here. Every loss sticks with me. It would have been a ridiculous day, had we won that football game. That night would have been magical. It was good as it was. It maybe would have been too storybook. That loss won't deter from that night, or my feelings. We accomplished a lot here for 16 years and we've been pretty consistent."

— ALVAREZ REFLECTING ON THE LOSS TO IOWA IN HIS FINAL HOME GAME IN 2005.

"If we're not successful in football, there's no Kohl Center, there's no boathouse, there's nothing. Knowing we had a part in all of that just makes me very proud."

— ALVAREZ AFTER ANNOUNCING HIS RETIREMENT FROM COACHING ON JULY 28, 2005.

"Our staff has been to big games, and I've been to big games. You didn't see our team tighten up, because that's the way we approached it. We didn't change one thing this week. If you change stuff, players get tense, coaches get tense. All you do is play how you've played all along."

—ALVAREZ AFTER CLINCHING HIS FIRST
ROSE BOWL TRIP WITH A 41–20
VICTORY OVER MICHIGAN STATE
ON DECEMBER 4, 1993, IN TOKYO.

"I don't know about you, but we're going to Disneyland. This football team would not be denied. This football team wanted to bring a Big Ten championship back to Madison and back to the state of Wisconsin. ... Let me just say this— Pasadena and California will not be the same after Wisconsin's through with it."

—ALVAREZ TO FANS AT PEP RALLY
ON DECEMBER 6, 1993,
AFTER RETURNING FROM TOKYO.

Barry Alvarez

Traditions and Pageantry

What is a college football Saturday without the pageantry? When it comes to the traditions and experiences that make college football so unique—unlike any other sport—the University of Wisconsin takes a back seat to no other school in the country.

Camp Randall Stadium traditionally gets voted as one of the best college stadiums in the nation, appearing on top 10 lists in *The Sporting News, SI on Campus* and Rivals.com. *The Indianapolis Star* named it the top stadium in the Big Ten.

But Wisconsin fans know there is a lot more to the college football experience than just the stadiums and the games.

"ON, WISCONSIN"

On, Minnesota? Just doesn't sound right, does it? But when the music was originally composed in 1909 by Chicago's William Purdy, he was going to submit the song for a $100 prize that the University of Minnesota was offering for a new football song.

Carl Beck, a fraternity brother of Purdy's at Hamilton College in Clinton, New York, had another idea. Beck, who was a roommate of Purdy's in Chicago, offered to write the words after hearing the music, then suggested they offer it to Wisconsin, where Beck once studied.

The song, which has come to be one of the most recognizable college fight songs, was an instant hit on campus and spread throughout the world. It was especially popular with military bands. Some 2,500 schools have adopted the music and changed the words to suit their needs. "On, Wisconsin" was sung for the first time at the 1909 homecoming game vs. Minnesota.

Current band director Michael Leckrone adapted the music in his first year in 1969. The original version had been played virtually unchanged since its inception. "I got a lot of flak for that," Leckrone said. "The old version was one you had to wait on. I wanted to generate immediate crowd reaction, so I stepped it up a bit."

On, Wisconsin

On, Wisconsin, On Wisconsin

Plunge right through that line,

Run the ball clear down

the field, boys

Touchdown sure this time

On Wisconsin, On Wisconsin

Fight on for her fame,

Fight, Fellows, Fight, Fight, Fight

We'll win this game!

BUCKY BADGER

While Badgers in various forms were recognized as the school mascot for decades, the current version, known as Bucky, sporting a cardinal-and-white letter sweater, was first drawn in 1940 by artist Art Evans. The badger went by names like Benny, Buddy, Bernie, Bobby and Bouncey. Art Lentz, the department's publicity director, had the idea to bring the mascot to life.

The original live badger mascot proved too vicious to control, often escaping handlers. It was decided in the interest of fan and player safety that Wisconsin's mascot be retired to the Madison Zoo. The Badger Yearbook replaced the live badger with a small raccoon named Regdab (badger backwards) and passed it off as a "badger in a raccoon coat."

In 1949 Connie Conrad, a student in the university's art department, was commissioned to mold a papier mâché badger head. Gymnast and cheerleader Bill Sagal, of Plymouth, Wisconsin, was directed by homecoming chair Bill Sachse to wear the outfit at the homecoming game.

A contest was staged to name the popular mascot. The winner was Buckingham U. Badger, or Bucky. The name apparently came from the lyrics in a song that encouraged the football team to "buck right through that line."

Bucky Badger has persevered through the years, even surviving a threat by then-assistant attorney general Howard Koop, in 1973. He suggested that Bucky be replaced by Henrietta Holstein, a loveable cow. Koop argued, "Kids love cows. A generation could grow up supporting the university and Henrietta Holstein." Koop's effort to overthrow Bucky failed. Thankfully.

COLORS

The Wisconsin Athletic Department's official colors are cardinal and white. PMS 200 is the designated color of the cardinal.

BADGER NICKNAME

The Badgers nickname was borrowed from the state of Wisconsin. The territory was dubbed the "Badger State," not because of an abundance of those animals in the region, but rather an association with lead miners in the 1820s. Prospectors came to the state looking for minerals. Without shelter in the winter, the miners had to "live like badgers" in tunnels burrowed into hillsides.

CAMP RANDALL STADIUM

Already regarded as one of the best college stadiums in the country, Camp Randall underwent a four-year, $109 million renovation prior to the 2005 season that drew wide praise for making the game-day experience even better for fans. The improvements included suites and club seats, video scoreboards, new offices, more restrooms and concession stands, as well as increased seating capacity to 80,321.

By enclosing the field, with the suites and offices on the east side and new seats filling in the bowl on the south end, the stadium also became appreciably louder. Now, noise from the upper deck on the west side "bounces off" the new three-story structure atop the east stands and reverberates around the stadium.

The enhanced environment also paid dividends on the field. From 2004 to 2006, the Badgers had an 18–1 record at home.

UW MARCHING BAND

The football team was not the only thing struggling in 1969. When Mike Leckrone arrived on campus late that summer, interest in the marching band was at an all-time low. The reasons for that were varied. Leckrone was the third director in three years, the football team was in the midst of a 23-game stretch without a victory and campuses across the country were experiencing protests and unrest. Wearing a uniform and marching around in a military manner were not popular activities among young people at the time.

But Leckrone changed that perception in a hurry, ushering in the greatest era in band history. He approached his job with unbridled enthusiasm, energy and new ideas. He introduced intense physical conditioning, requiring all prospective band members to attend fundamental drills during registration week. He developed a more demanding marching stride ("Stop at the Top"), a new emphasis on showmanship, a new pregame entrance ("The Run-on") and above all, he expected Marching Band "to be fun."

In the years to follow, the marching band led the way when it came to having fun—sometimes, too much fun. With its popular postgame celebrations and impromptu concerts—like the one that snarled traffic after a 1978 NCAA hockey semifinal game in Providence, Rhode Island—and overall craziness, the UW Marching Band quickly built a national reputation for its creativity, as well as its music.

In 2006 the marching band went too far and UW chancellor John Wiley put it on probation for "vulgar behavior" on a road trip to Ann Arbor, Michigan, but that likely only served to add to its reputation as the craziest band in the land.

BAND CAPS

When a Badger team wins an athletic contest, members of the band turn their hats around and wear them backwards. The practice started in the 1920s to symbolize the band looking back at the victory in days when they marched out with the departing crowd.

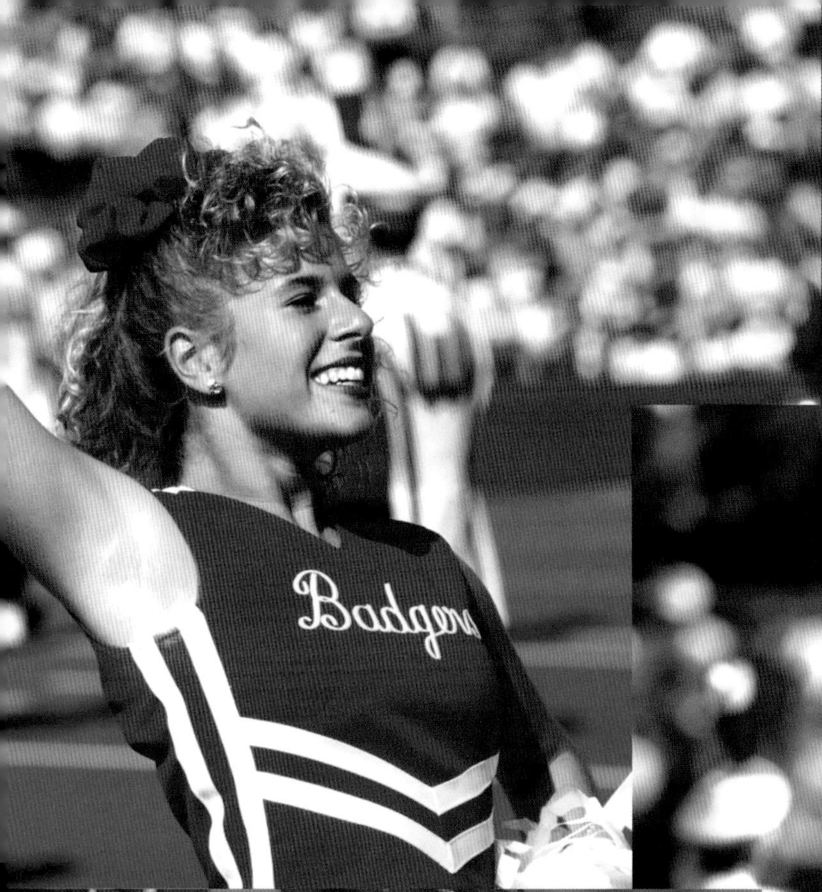

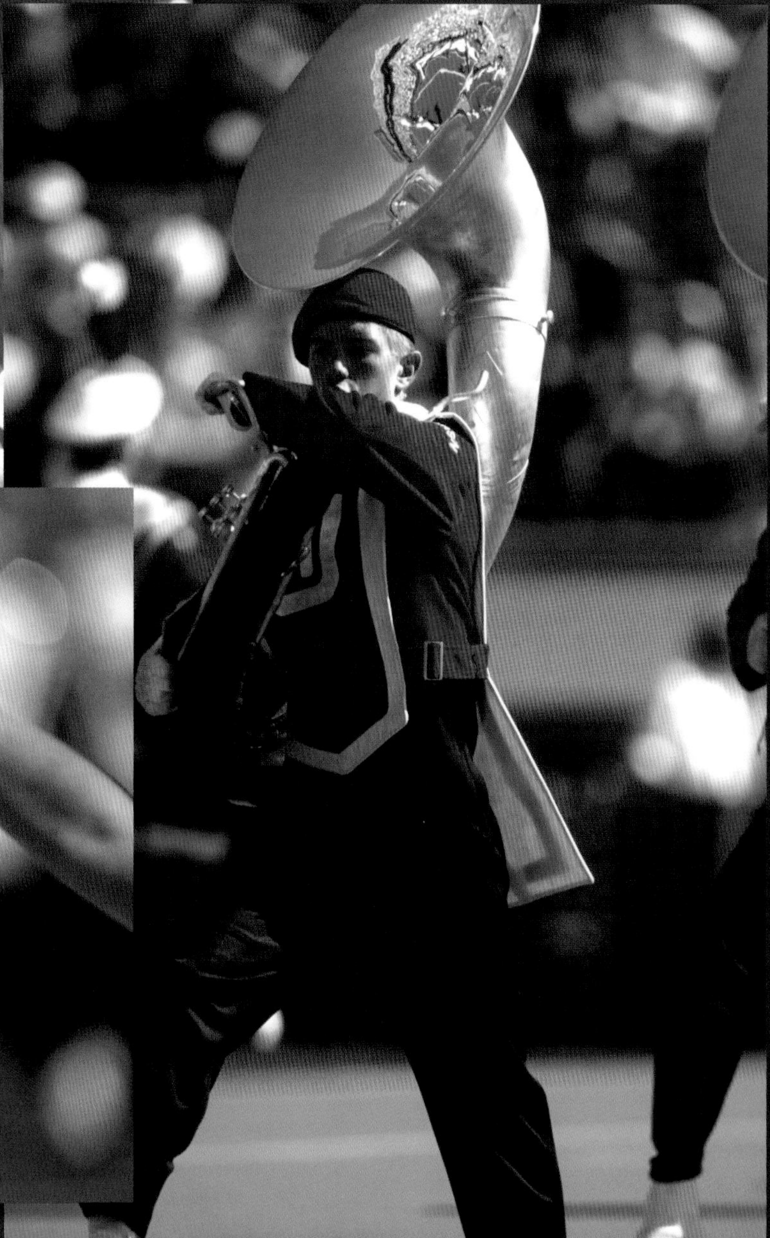

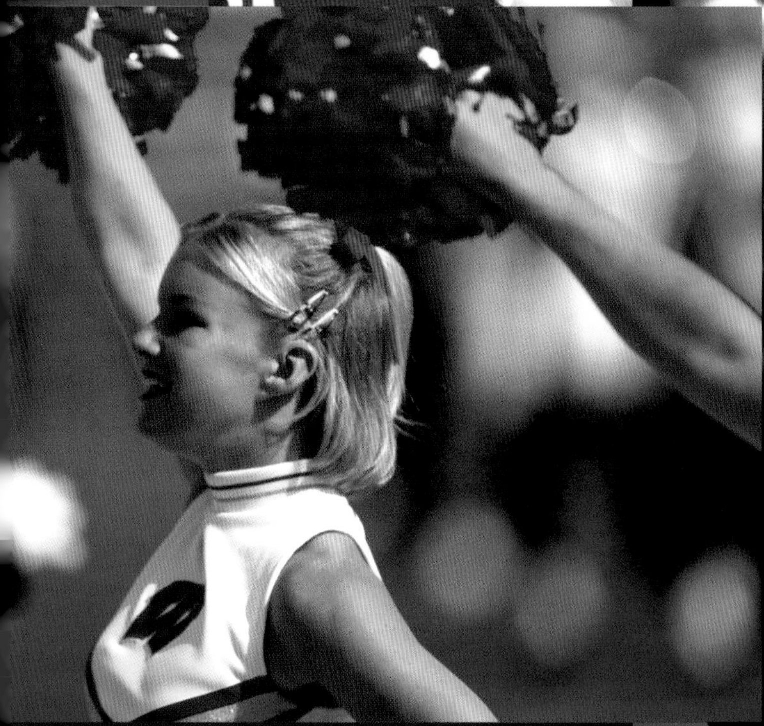

BUD SONG

An integral part of any Wisconsin band performance is the playing of the Bud song. The tune is a spinoff of the song "You've Said it All," a jingle with words and music originally written by Steve Karmen for Budweiser beer commercials. Copyrighted by Sandlee Publishing Corporation in 1970, the song has become legendary among fans because of its polka-like rhythm.

Band director Michael Leckrone said the song's popularity got started at a 1975 hockey game. "The crowd wanted to hear a polka," he said. "I didn't have any polkas. We had, just by accident, this beer commercial in the tunes we play. I told the band if we substituted the word 'Wisconsin' for 'Budweiser' it would work."

Leckrone said the song became a football tradition after a 1978 come-from-behind victory over Oregon. "Wisconsin was behind by three touchdowns, and the crowd was really dead," he said. "I played the song to get everyone pepped up. About 20 seconds after that, Wisconsin scored a TD. I played it again, and Wisconsin scored another touchdown. From then on, the band could never play enough 'Bud.'"

FIFTH QUARTER

The Wisconsin band has become nationally famous for its postgame celebration called "the Fifth Quarter." Win or lose, thousands of fans stick around to sing, dance and cheer with the band as they play traditional favorites, like "On, Wisconsin" and the Bud song. Originally, the postgame concert was designed to give fans something to listen to on their way out of the stadium, but it developed into a postgame party as the band built in audience participation activities.

"VARSITY"

The traditional arm-waving at the end of the song, "Varsity," done to the words "U-rah-rah, Wis-con-sin," was the 1934 brainstorm of band leader Ray Dvorak. He saw Pennsylvania students wave their caps after losing a game. Dvorak later instructed Wisconsin students to salute UW President Glenn Frank after each game.

The words:

Var-sity! Var-sity! U-rah-rah! Wisconsin!

Praise to thee we sing

Praise to thee our Alma Mater

U-rah-rah, Wisconsin!

"JUMP AROUND"

Between the third and fourth quarters of every home game, thousands of Wisconsin fans, band members and usually several football players—including a few from the opposing team—jump in unison to the 1990s hip-hop tune by House of Pain, which literally causes the entire stadium to rock and the upper deck to sway.

"It's hard to hear yourself think," former Penn State quarterback Michael Robinson said of playing in Camp Randall Stadium. "And when they play 'Jump Around,' you can feel the place shake. It gets pretty loud and crazy."

GRADUATING LAW STUDENTS

At the homecoming game, graduating law students throw canes over the crossbar of the goal post in a pregame ceremony. If students catch their cane, legend claims they will win their first case. If the cane is dropped, the case will be lost. The custom originated at Harvard and came to the UW in 1910.

MOTION "W"

When Barry Alvarez came to Madison in 1990, he decided the helmet logo needed to be updated to signal a new era in Wisconsin football. He entertained 15 to 20 different designs before Rayovac artist Rick Suchanek developed the "Motion W," which included a tail at the back of the logo. Alvarez thought the tail was a bit much, but when it was removed, decided to go with it. The university bought the rights to the design, and the logo has been adopted by all other UW sports.

PORTAGE PLUMBER

Terry Westegard was working as a steam fitter in Portage, Wisconsin, when he made his first appearance in front of the crowd at a Wisconsin football game in 1976. Wearing a fur skirt and helmet, Westegard came running out of Section X to perform with the pompon squad as it made its way around the stadium.

The first time he did it, he was motivated by fans in his section and a few shots of tequila. The crowd's response was so encouraging he continued his routine at each home game, acquiring his costume and his nickname as he went along.

"That was back when things were a little rowdier," Westegard said in a 1991 interview with the *Wisconsin State Journal*. "It seemed like the next thing to do. I saw the girls coming around the corner, and I had already had the attention of a lot of people in my section, so I went down and got on the end of the line and just did it."

Although the coaches were not big fans of the routine, Westegard helped entertain crowds at a time when Wisconsin ranked among the leaders in the nation in attendance, but winning seasons were rare. He retired at the end of the 1981 season, when the Badgers went 7–5 and football started to take center stage again.

"It wasn't as spontaneous as it used to be," Westegard said. "It became more like a thing I had to do instead of something that was fun to do."

ARTIFICIAL TURF

Due mostly to a shortage of grass practice fields in the area and heavy usage of the field, Camp Randall Stadium has had artificial turf since 1968, when Wisconsin became the second school in the country to install Tartan Turf.

Designed by the 3M Company, the original turf cost $210,000 and was funded by the UW Parking and Transportation Board in exchange for permission to convert practice fields on the north end of Camp Randall into a 500-car parking lot.

The initial surface turned black in some areas when the green fiber tips broke off, so 3M sprayed the field green for the 1969 season. Many players grew to hate the surface, which was as firm as cement and abrasive, leading to ugly "rug burns."

It was replaced prior to Wisconsin's 1998 Big Ten championship season. At the same time, the school replaced the playing surface in the McClain Athletic Center, too.

During the summer of 2003, Wisconsin contracted with FieldTurf, which had become the playing surface of choice for a number of major college and professional stadiums. The turf includes a sand and ground-up rubber base that leads to excellent drainage in wet conditions and a soft, non-abrasive condition to cushion falls. Yardage numerals and hash marks are glued in, and the red end zone names and center Motion W were manufactured according to UW color specs and added in the fall of 2004.

Pete Monty is the career leader in tackles.

Facts and Figures

CAREER STATISTICAL LEADERS

- Rushes: 1,220, Ron Dayne, 1996–1999
- Rushing Yards: 7,125, Ron Dayne, 1996–1999
- Passing Attempts: 1,052, Darrell Bevell, 1992–1995
- Completions: 646, Darrell Bevell, 1992–1995
- Passing Yardage: 7,686, Darrell Bevell, 1992–1995
- Completion Percentage: .614, Darrell Bevell, 1992–1995
- Touchdown Passes: 59, Darrell Bevell, 1992–1995
- Receptions: 175, Lee Evans, 1999–2003
- Receiving Yardage: 3,468, Lee Evans, 1999–2003
- Receiving Touchdowns: 26, Lee Evans, 1999–2003
- Total Offense: 7,477, Darrell Bevell, 1992–1995
- Punt Return Average: 12.8, Jim Leonhard, 2001–2004
- Kickoff Return Average: 24.6, Greg Johnson, 1969, 1971
- Punting Average: 43.5, Kevin Stemke, 1997–2000
- Scoring: 426, Ron Dayne, 1996–1999
- Interceptions: 21, Jamar Fletcher, 1999–2000; Jim Leonhard, 2001–2004
- Tackles: 451, Pete Monty, 1993–1996
- Sacks: 33, Tarek Saleh, 1993–1996
- Tackles for Loss: 283, Tarek Saleh, 1993–1996

*John Stocco in the
2007 Capital One Bowl.*

ALL-TIME BOWL GAME SCORES

Bowl	Date	Result
Rose	1953	Southern Cal 7, Wisconsin 0
Rose	1960	Washington 44, Wisconsin 8
Rose	1963	Southern Cal 42, Wisconsin 37
Garden State	1981	Tennessee 28, Wisconsin 21
Independence	1982	Wisconsin 14, Kansas State 3
Hall of Fame	1984	Kentucky 20, Wisconsin 19
Rose	1994	Wisconsin 21, UCLA 16
Hall of Fame	1995	Wisconsin 34, Duke 20
Copper	1996	Wisconsin 38, Utah 10
Outback	1998	Georgia 33, Wisconsin 6
Rose	1999	Wisconsin 38, UCLA 31
Rose	2000	Wisconsin 17, Stanford 9
Sun	2000	Wisconsin 21, UCLA 20
Alamo	2002	Wisconsin 31, Colorado 28
Music City	2003	Auburn 28, Wisconsin 14
Outback	2005	Georgia 24, Wisconsin 21
Capital One	2006	Wisconsin 24, Auburn 10
Capital One	2007	Wisconsin 17, Arkansas 14

Overall

Won 10, Lost 8, Tied 0

BADGERS IN THE COLLEGE FOOTBALL HALL OF FAME

Name	Position	Years	Inducted
Alan Ameche	Fullback	1951–1954	1975
Marty Below	Tackle	1922–1923	1988
Bob Butler	Tackle	1911–1913	1972
Pat Harder	Fullback	1941–1942	1993
Elroy Hirsch	Halfback	1942	1974
George Little	Coach	1925–1926	1955
Pat O'Dea	Fullback/Punter/Kicker	1896–1899	1962
Pat Richter	End	1960–1962	1996
Dave Schreiner	End	1940–1942	1955

CONSENSUS ALL-AMERICANS

1912	Robert "Butts" Butler, T
1913	Ray "Tubby" Keeler, G
1915	Howard "Cub" Buck, T
1919	Charles Carpenter, C
1920	Ralph Scott, T
1923	Marty Below, T
1930	Milo Lubratovich, T
1942	Dave Schreiner, E
1954	Alan Ameche, FB
1959	Dan Lanphear, T
1962	Pat Richter, E
1975	Dennis Lick, T
1981	Tim Krumrie, DL
1994	Cory Raymer, C
1998	Aaron Gibson, T
1998	Tom Burke, DE
1999	Ron Dayne, TB
1999	Chris McIntosh, T
2000	Jamar Fletcher, CB
2004	Erasmus James, DE
2006	Joe Thomas, T

BADGERS IN THE PRO FOOTBALL HALL OF FAME

Elroy "Crazylegs" Hirsch, E
Inducted 1968
Chicago Rockets, 1946–1948
Los Angeles Rams, 1949–1957
- Totaled 387 receptions for 7,029 yards and 60 touchdowns in pro career
- Key figure in Rams' revolutionary three-end offense in 1949

Mike Webster, C
Inducted 1997
Pittsburgh Steelers, 1974–1988
Kansas City Chiefs, 1989–1990
- Played more seasons (15) and more games (220) than any other player in Steelers history
- Nine-time Pro Bowl pick, including five as a starter
- Won four Super Bowls with the Steelers
- Had a streak of 150 consecutive starts between 1976 and 1986

NATIONAL AWARD WINNERS

Award	Player	Year
Heisman	Alan Ameche	1954
Heisman	Ron Dayne	1999
Maxwell	Ron Dayne	1999
Walter Camp	Alan Ameche	1953
Walter Camp	Ron Dayne	1999
Doak Walker	Ron Dayne	1999
Outland	Joe Thomas	2006
Ray Guy	Kevin Stemke	2000
Jim Thorpe	Jamar Fletcher	2000

RETIRED NUMBERS

33*	Ron Dayne
35	Alan Ameche
40	Elroy Hirsch
80	Dave Schreiner
83	Allan Shafer
88	Pat Richter

*not retired but not assigned since Dayne's final season

Ron Dayne